LANDED ON THE MOON

Johnny Mack was born in Peckham, South-East London, an only child to loving but strict parents. In the first volume of his memoirs, *Dunpeckham,* he described his indoctrination into the criminal fraternity and his life of crime, violence, addiction and prison. In *Landed on the Moon* Johnny recounts his efforts to change his way of life after being swindled in an unsuccessful scam in London. As such, he moved to the Isle of Wight to start a new life. However, when he arrived there from the city mean streets, he felt like such an outsider, it was as if he had landed on the moon. He used all his resourcefulness to provide for himself and his loyal wife and family in ways that were not always legitimate. This, his second book, is told with the same earthiness and brutal honesty that characterised *Dunpeckham* but with an added poignancy. Johnny found that in order to gain the peace of mind that had always eluded him, he had to lose almost everything.

**Published Work:**

**Dunpeckham (2008)**
*Olympia Publishers*
ISBN: 9781905513505

# LANDED ON THE MOON

**Johnny Mack**

# LANDED ON THE MOON

Olympia Publishers
*London*

**www.olympiapublishers.com**
OLYMPIA PAPERBACK EDITION

A CIP catalogue record for this title is
available from the British Library.

ISBN: 978-1-84897-153-0

Cover design by Graham Gauntlett

First Published in 2011

## Dedication

To my beloved Mum and Dad

&

Billy who stopped H from shooting me

# Acknowledgments

I would like to express my sincere gratitude to my ex-wife, Carol.

She went through all the madness I created in my life and it was her that I owe my life to. Through the madness she maintained a level of sanity and helped beat my demons by standing by me and at the same time being a fantastic mother bringing up our children.

I wish to express a special thank you to my editorial assistant, Guy Robinson, who has become a very good friend and has helped me so much in the production of this book.

A special thank you goes out to Chris Evans of EDC New Media Solutions Ltd. For his faith and appreciation in me for my hard work and for getting my work out there for the public to see. A special thank you to Rachele Wiggins for her input in getting extra publicity.

A very special thank you goes to Lee Hutcheon and Anoushaka of Clans films, who have guided me and continuously backed me all along with my writing. Along with John Pettigrew who has put me in touch with some amazing people.

# Sinner to 'Saint'

I've made a new friend, a very special friend

Who in his youth, went along with the trend


The estate he lived on, wasn't the best

It was rough and ready and I do not jest


Trouble was rife, fights on the street

Joining in, as he would not be beat


Sometimes things, got out of control

People got hurt, things took their toll


It came to a head, enough was enough

Time to change, though the decision was tough


He became a boxer, even turned pro

Changing his ways, it really did show


Change we all can, but for how long

To keep it up, you have to be strong

Only time would tell, if he was to succeed

Learning your lesson, are wise words to heed


Well, so far so good, twenty-seven years on

From sinner to 'saint' is proof that he's won


He now spends his time, helping others succeed

Using his knowledge, writing novels to read


An inspiration, to each and everyone

That if you try hard enough, it can be done


Believe it or not, we haven't even met

I've not read his book, well not yet


In my opinion, he can hold his head up high

The story he tells, brings a tear to my eye

# I

# "LEAVING"

I looked at a grey asbestos shed. 'What the bloody hell is this, babe? You told me that we had a nice little white cottage with a thatched roof, a nice garden, and red roses around the bloody front door, Carol. This is a post war shed sweetheart! Not a bloody cottage! I wouldn't put a fucking dog in it, let alone a family, Fuck me!' My voice now raised I carried on at Carol. 'What are you playing at? What's going on? Why all the bullshit?' and I just carried on yelling and effing and blinding until I had Carol in tears.

As I stopped the tirade of whining and moaning, I looked just over her shoulder and saw two of my three kids standing in the doorway looking at me with those same confused eyes and blank expressions on their faces, the same faces that would look at me when I used to come back to our flat in Peckham after having a bad day with no money or drugs, shouting and hollering, that same look that would now create shame and fear in me.

The day had started with a miserable nightmare of a journey; it was a poxy January day, and it was fucking snowing, and freezing, and I had the hump up to my eyebrows. I had just left Peckham for what I thought would be the last time; it had taken me a long time to accept that I had to leave the area, the area where I was born, the area where I became street-wise and educated to fight the system, and the same area where I had done my apprenticeship in the world of villainy. It was my home, I knew nothing else; outside Peckham was alien to me, anyone from outside a 3-mile radius was considered untrustworthy, unreliable and probably a grass, and they were the rules I worked to. I knew no different; I'd been taught that if I played the game, I could be sure that I would come out a winner and earn respect, but if I fucked up, I would expect my losses would involve losing not only my respect, but something very precious to me, and I have always thought of my life as being quite precious.

Carol had moved (escaped) to the Isle of Wight with the kids and had been staying with my Mum and Dad. They had got out of Peckham three years before, just prior to the race riots (thank God). Peckham was not the same for them and the people were now different, and it had lost a lot of its character, but above all, they felt unsafe. When I was a kid, I remember the old boys up the market, each one of them was a character and everyone knew everyone and everyone trusted everyone. I used to see the dodgy deals going on and the expertise of these geezers when they were at their work – they could sell fucking sand to the Arabs. It was a different place in the fifties through to the seventies but it started to change once the council housing estates started springing up everywhere. They later became a breeding ground for every low life scumbag you could imagine; gangs, drugs, prostitution, you name it, the estates would breed it, and this was the place which, ironically, I didn't want to leave. Carol on the other hand wanted out of Peckham for the sake of our kids; after all, she had seen what Peckham had done to me and did not want the same for the kids.

She had arrived at my parents' place with the kids about three months prior to my arrival and told them that she could not go on living the way we were living and asked to stay. Mum and Dad loved Carol and the kids and only wanted the best for them, so they took them in, whereas I was still under the illusion that I could not survive outside my manor. I had just conquered my drug habit and started working as a taxi driver and avoided all my old haunts. We had previously tried living outside London just after I kicked my drug habit – I had got myself back into shape and was earning a living from prize fighting, but even that did not go the way we had planned and I signed on the dole and started living life as one of the four million, but after a while I convinced Carol that living like that was not for me and went back to Peckham alone. In a short space of time I started getting involved with my old pals, who were still at it with the villainy. I tried very hard to stay away, but every time I saw my mates they were flaunting their proceeds from crime and living the dream, and I was earning if I was lucky fifteen quid a week on the dole, and it was this that started me thinking that maybe I could get involved with one last score and then move out of the area.

One of my pals was a sound geezer called Harry or H as we called him. I had been on a number of blags with him in the late seventies and we worked well together. I trusted him completely and he was a genius with electrics and alarms, whereas me, I could just about put a battery in a radio. H now ran a little firm over in Bermondsey and word had it that he was on the lookout for another body for a bit of work over in the city. I called in to his local – The Fort – just off Grange Road, Bermondsey and found him in a darkened alcove at the back of the boozer with three other geezers and a couple of old tarts. H always had a bird on his arm even though he was married with three kids; he never took his old woman out and always gave the impression that he was single. He was a good-looking geezer about six three and built like a brick shithouse, he had thick black wavy hair and the women loved him. As I got close to his little crowd, a Popeye-type arm, complete with tattoos, came in front of me from the bar area and stopped me in my tracks. I looked round to see who the owner was of this piece of meat and I was confronted with Billy, my old partner in crime, who I had thought was still inside.

Billy grinned and said, 'You fucking wanker, what are you?'

I said, 'Hello Bill, what you done, fucking escaped?' and with that Billy lets out a fucking big roar and bear-hugs me and starts trying to fucking kiss me.

'Fuck off, you fucking psycho, you could have cleaned your fucking teeth, your breath smells like a horse's arse.' Just as I was going to give Billy some more abuse, a hand rests on my shoulder and as I turned, H was in front of me.

'Hello Macky boy. I heard you was back on the manor – come sit down and have a drink and a chat,' and with that Billy came and sat with us. After a few formalities, H tells the girls to clear off and got Chris who was his right hand man to get the drinks in. As I was supping my pint, H looks me straight in the eyes as if he was an optician and then he grabs my arm tightly and pulls my sleeve up around my elbow.

'What's up, H?'

'I had a whisper, Mack, that you were on the gear,' and as he was talking he was turning my arm, obviously looking for track marks or some sign of drug abuse. Armed robbery, thieving, or fraud or in some cases murder were acceptable to H, but if you were a drug user then in his mind you could not be trusted and you would be cast out as a leper would be back in the middle ages.

Billy butted in and said, 'He's not a user, H,' with a completely straight face. Bill then looked me straight in the eyes and said, 'you're not a skaghead, are you, John?'

Calmly I said, 'No, Bill, I'm not a skaghead.'

H then went on to tell me what he had heard through the grapevine. I cut him short when I told him that I had set up quite a few skag dealers so as to be able to rob them, and to do that properly, I had to let them think that I was a user, and because of that, word had got out that I was a user.

There was a silence, short, but it seemed to go on for ages, then H said, 'Well, that's alright then, just checking,' then everybody started laughing, but I knew H would watch me like a hawk from then on.

I arranged to meet H later that week, I had told him that I was looking for some work and I gave him the run-down on what I had been doing. I explained that after the blags on the dealers, I left London with Carol and the kids for a while to let things die down. H knew that drug dealers had no morals and probably would have gone after Carol and the kids if they couldn't have got me, so my story and absence from the scene made sense to him. If he had found out that I had lied, I would have been fucked, and it was just as well that no one really knew about my ex-habit, but I had no choice, I needed money and the only way was for me to go back to work. I only wanted one last score, so the work would have to be worthwhile. I would also have to give the impression that I was to be about for a while and not let anyone know my intentions or plans.

I met H that week at his sister's place; it was much safer than going to his house, because there was a good chance that his gaff would be on 'obbo' from the local old bill. When I arrived Billy and Chris were already there along with a fat middle-aged foreign geezer who I did not know. H introduced me to the fat geezer, 'Mack, this is Assam. Assam, this is Mack.' There was small talk amongst us until H said, 'Alright boys, let's get down to business,' and with that Assam told us about a scam he was involved with, then about how he had been double-crossed by his business partner, who happened to be his cousin. The scam was to smuggle in gold Krugerands from South Africa and then resell them here, but with V.A.T. added. They had a near foolproof way of getting the coins into this country, and once here, they knew a way for them to become legit tender and sell them on the open market. I sat there and listened tentatively and thought to myself that if I am asked to smuggle in this gold, then they could take a fucking run and jump; I wasn't a smuggler, just one look at my menacing face going through customs would give the game away.

H then piped up and asked Assam to explain what happened with one shipment that was landed a few months ago. Assam explained to us that his cousin and he had arranged for £250,000 worth of merchandise to be brought into this country. Now, both Assam and the cousin had been putting up the dough for this operation and had been working it for near on a year with no problems, until the last shipment. They had arranged a courier to pick the shipment up from the person who had brought the KGs into the country. They only ever used legit courier companies and never used the same one twice, so there was little chance of anyone getting familiar with the run, but on that occasion their courier had been run off his bike out in the suburbs and the shipment stolen, leaving poor old Assam and his cousin a quarter million plus seventeen and a half percent out of pocket, (sounds sad don't it – now that's what I would call a nice pucker touch, given the chance). Assam then told us about his cousin's financial situation, which consisted of £150,000 of gambling debts and he was going through a costly and messy divorce back in the States. Well, you don't have to be Einstein to work out that the cousin had tucked up Assam and then fronted it, as Assam mentioned that, with no proof he could not even suggest to his cousin that he had had him over. Apart from that, it would have caused ructions in their family if he had accused him with no proof, so Assam gave him the impression that he believed that they had been tucked up, probably by someone from the African connection.

It had been a few months since the last shipment and Assam's cousin had been out of the country on the pretence that he was sorting his messy divorce out, but it was probably more like him spending Assam's money the slippery bastard. H piped up and asked us all if we had any ideas; Billy was the type of geezer who was limited on grey matter but had plenty of brawn, and Chris was a yes man, but give credit where it's due, they were both loyal and totally trustworthy, so really the question was being directed at me.

I said to H, 'Can I have a quick word in the kitchen?' and we both got up and left Billy and Chris with Assam. When we were on our own, I told H that I only wanted in on this if Assam was kept in the dark about our impending plan and whatever we came up with, he was only to be given limited knowledge.

H gave me a meaningful look and said, 'Don't trust him, do you Mack?'

I said, 'Well, put it this way, H. I've never met the geezer before today and I don't mean to be disrespectful, but I have never trusted foreigners and he looks as dodgy as fuck, so the less he knows, the better.'

With that, H leans over and gives me a hug. 'Would you feel better if we spoke alone tomorrow? Just you and me?'

'H, that would suit me fine,' I said, relieved that he understood me, 'and I need to know all you got on these characters, Assam and his so called partner.'

H said, 'That's what I love about you, Mack, you trust no one.'

'That's why I'm not banged up, H,' I said seriously and asked him to give me a bell later at my brother-in-law's home and left without saying goodbye to the others.

That night I went for a drink at my local, The Marlborough Head, in Goldsmith Road, Peckham, still thinking about the bit of work that H was providing. I needed a decent score because I was skint and I needed to send money to Carol and the kids on the Isle of Wight. I was staying with my brother-in-law, Les, who was a really straight bloke and would do anything for me, but I felt in the way at his house; after all, Les helped me when I came off the skag, he and his wife put me up and fed me until I was well again. He also had four kids and with me in the way, he couldn't have a proper family life, so I needed to sort out a decent earner and get the fuck out of Peckham, to start living a new and proper life with Carol and the kids and to do that I had to have cash. I had promised Carol faithfully that I would give up the skull-duggery once I got clean from the drugs, and move away to start afresh, but the truth was that I was shit scared of the thought of not being able to earn a living, and the thought of moving out of my manor was the equivalent of emigrating to Australia. I kept giving Carol excuses, but she got tired of my bullshit and told me that she was adamant about moving her and the kids out to the Isle of Wight with or without me. The thought of being away from them frightened me; after all, they were my life, and I needed them to be close, so as to protect them. I needed the work that H was offering, but most important the work had to be well paid, because it would have to set me up, or at least give me a decent start.

I got the phone call from H; we arranged a meet out of the manor, away from prying eyes. It's always a good idea, when you're about to work with someone not to be seen in public together, because believe me, there is many a scum bag grass out there willing to pass that info onto the flying squad for their intelligence. Then, if by a bit of bad luck one of you gets caught on a bit of work, then the other one is pretty safe because the old bill have no Intel. I was always cautious. I couldn't afford not to be; I was in a dog-eat-dog business. An old con I met in Wormwood Scrubs years ago, gave me some sound advice, regarding the criminal fraternity – 'Trust everyone you work with, but never trust the devil inside them.' – That made sense to me and I used it every time I went to work.

I turned up at the meet and H was already there, sitting in a builders' truck with a hard hat on, ladders, cement mixer, the works, supping a coffee from a thermos flask.

The first words I said were, 'Fucking shrewd cover, H. I like it, mate. No one would dream of looking out for you in that thing.'

'Macky boy, I can go anywhere in this. Who takes any notice of a builder's truck?'

I said, 'H, let's talk shop. What did you find out about Assam and his cousin?'

H said, with a crafty grin, 'Found out quite a bit, Mack.' Then there's this silence from him. He had a fucking habit of doing this; I had known him long enough to know that silence, with that grin, meant some sort of good news.

'Fuck's sake, H. What's the S.P. on these two monkeys?'

'Better than I thought, Mack. Assam is on the level, about his cousin. He has skanked him good and proper, but he's not working it alone.'

I'm all ears now. 'Who's he working with?'

'The prick is working with a diplomat!'

'Diplomat? What fucking diplomat?'

'The same fucking diplomat that's been bringing in the KGs.'

I went quiet, absorbed what H had just said and then my brain went into overdrive.

'That grey matter of yours must be working overtime, Mack, but there's more mate. Wait till you hear the full S.P., and then put that brain of yours into gear.'

'Okay, H, fire away mate.'

H told me that the diplomat had been bringing in not only the KGs but Charlie (cocaine) as well for another crew. As it turned out, this little firm wasn't too happy with the quality of their merchandise once it arrived in the U.K, so the fucking Diplomat must have been cutting the gear and replacing what he's taken with milk powder or some crap like that. This was music to my ears, and a plan was coming together already. H told me all he had found out about the diplomat and the other firm he was doing business with, via a source who owed him a favour. I told H that I needed time to come up with a plan and I'd be in touch in a few days.

I loved this part of the 'work' – it's not all fucking gung ho and sticking a shooter in some poor unfortunate innocent prick's mouth and yelling, 'Give us the dough, you cunt!' You had to use your loaf, have a plan, then another plan to cover your arse if it went pear-shaped. What H had told me gave me plenty of scope for ideas; that's why I was on this one. H knew I was good at doing this type of planning and he also knew I wouldn't take too many risks or want to use excessive violence. Going to extremes with violence could double a prison sentence if caught and anyway, deep down I hated using it and only used it when I had too. I had always planned my work with a touch of scare-mongering, with a bit of psychology thrown in; it had worked for me in the past, so why change what works. My only problem was planning things with Billy's involvement, because he was a fucking lunatic and would sooner shoot you, to get want he wanted and then fuck off, no plan at all. Billy was never a planner, he was just muscle with a big fucking frightening face, mixed with an evil, scary personality, which would without doubt scare the shit out of anyone when he was working, but he was a fucking liability when it came down to violence, he just seemed to get off on it. Apart from that he was a loyal, staunch and trusted geezer, so I had to put him in a position on this piece of work where he could be controlled and do less damage. Billy and I had worked together many times before, and on one occasion he had put me into a situation where I had to replace live ammunition with blanks just so that he didn't blow some poor fucker's head off, so Billy had to be watched and worked, in a way that he wouldn't notice too much.

In the mean time, I belled my Mum and Dad to let them know that I was fine, free from drugs and working. This of course was part true, but my Mother, bless her, had an uncanny way of knowing if I was speaking the truth or not. It was obvious from the sound of my voice, that I was drug free – that was a blessing to her, so she never went into interrogation mode. I explained that I would be over in a short time to be with Carol and the kids and was getting some dough together by working all hours as a mini-cab driver, so we could start afresh away from Peckham. Whether she believed me or not I'll never know. Her real main concern for me was that I stay clean of the crack and heroin and that I would get myself to the Island ASAP to be with Carol and the kids. They had been allocated a cottage by the council by this time, in a place called East Cowes, very close to where Queen Victoria had had a palace, Osborne House, and the area was full of yachtie's. It all sounded very countrified and dignified to me, but it scared the shit out of me, because I would have to leave Peckham and completely change my life-style and find new pals. After all, who the fuck did I know on the Isle of Wight, apart from those doing bird in Parkhurst? What would I do? The only thing that kept driving me on was that I wanted to be with my wife and kids; they came first, Mum and Dad a close second, and to be able to do this I had to have money.

I contacted H after a few days and asked him if he could get hold of the private address of our dodgy diplomat; not the address where Assam and his cousin were meeting him. All these dodgy diplomats had a flat or apartment somewhere, which only a few would know about, the sort of place where these fuckers would take call girls or do their illegal business transactions. After all they had to be careful as well, and most of these greedy fuckers were in office for only a short time, so they would milk the system in what time they had, probably to set themselves up once they were back in their native country or buy an island somewhere.

H didn't see it would be much of a problem, because he knew one of the crew who were dealing with the diplomat in the cocaine racket. I did say to H to be shrewd in obtaining the info, as it would be important at this stage not to draw to much attention. I told him that I had a plan in progress and would give him the full S.P as soon as he got the address

He said, 'Give us a few days, Mack, and we'll make a meet.'

I told him I'd wait to hear from him. What I was planning was quite simple and if all went well we should walk away not only with KGs, but maybe a few kilos of coke, which was £25,000 a kilo at that time. But most of all, we would walk away without any come-back and everyone would be none the wiser that our little firm had done the bit of work. This is where the other firm came into it; my idea was to put the bit of work down to them, which would convince Assam's dodgy cousin that he had been had over by another firm who was connected to the diplomat. Remember, Assam's cousin knew fuck all about the diplomat's other dodgy dealings. His understanding was that it was just him and Assam dealing with the diplomat – after all, you can only get so much into a diplomat's bag.

H contacted me and a meet was made in a safe house, North of the of the river. I fucking hated North London, always have done, must have rubbed off on to me from my old man, because he was of the same mind. The only good thing about the place is that I could guarantee that no-one would know me there. For this meet, I went by public transport just to be extra safe, took a bus, then the underground – the tube had saved my arse from getting nicked more times than I can remember, once you're underground you can just vanish, it was too fucking hard for the old bill to find you, let alone catch you. That's all changed today what with the Transport police and CCTV; they've got you covered once you enter any tube station, it's all down to these terrorist threats. London is just one big open prison, can't even take a dump without some fucking nerd sitting in a control room some three miles away looking up your arse with his high-tech camera. Why these so called criminals do what they do on the streets, knowing that they could be seen or filmed baffles me, the thick bastards, but one thing I am sure of is that most are pissed and haven't got a clue what they're doing, or they are drug users dying for a fix and just don't give a fuck.

Got to the safe house and H let me in. 'What you reckon, Macky boy?'

'H, you surprise me all the time mate, must have been that last bit of bird you done that's made you be so careful these days.'

H just replied, 'Once bitten, twice shy.' In other words, H had probably learnt a valuable lesson from his last sentence, and that is take the time to make the effort to keep safe from the Old Bill, so say nothing to no-one that doesn't need to be told, and keep your business to yourself, just keep your mouth shut, as easy as that. Most criminal faces have made the mistake of letting their ego get above the basic rules in this dog-eat-dog business and ended up coming unstuck, me included. I never asked H how he came across this safe house or how he got the use of it, because it was none of my business, so we sat down with a cuppa and I asked him if he had got the dodgy address of the diplomat.

'Got it mate and it's in Knightsbridge. Got Chris over there right now keeping obbo on the gaff, just to see what this dodgy fucker is up too. What's your plan Mack?'

I told H the plan about using the other firm; he liked it. I also told H that I was sure the diplomat was bringing into the country not only Assam's KGs but the other firm's cocaine at the same time and in the same bag. We needed Assam and his shit-bag of a cousin to arrange another shipment as quickly as possible. With that H stops me in mid flow and tells me that through his source, he had found out the other firm had nearly run out of their Charlie so they would want another shipment as soon as possible.

There was complete silence between us with both of us looking into thin air or looking at the carpet for what seemed ages. I myself wanted some feedback from H; I knew him well enough to know that he had his own plan and he was thinking whether mine was more operable then his own.

Then the silence was broken with H making what seemed more like a decision than a comment. 'I like this Mack; I know where you're coming from. What you're saying to me is we go in on the diplomat after his return with the goods, using a front story by telling him that we have been sent by the other firm to sort out a little problem that he has, regarding the purity of their client's merchandise.'

I said to H, 'Listen mate, we could also walk away with not only all the Charlie and KGs, but for all we know he may be smuggling in diamonds, especially from his part of the world. Who knows mate, it could be an Aladdin's cave inside that penthouse, but what we can guarantee is that the KGs and the Charlie will be there. Anything else is a bonus. H totally agreed with the plan and we left it that H would tell Assam to get in touch with his cousin to get another shipment ordered and keep the diplomat's penthouse under obbo and without saying nothing, not even Chris or Billy would know our plan, just the two of us.

H appeared at my brother-in-law's house a few days later, the fucker turned up at 4 a.m. and woke everyone with his banging on the door. When I opened the front door H was a right mess and burst in pushing me out of the way and went straight into the kitchen. Within seconds my brother and sister-in-law came downstairs screaming the odds about the commotion. I quickly put some clothes on, told my in-laws a load of bollocks that he had just split up with his missus, just so to keep them sweet and then grabbed H and took him out to my car and sat him in the passenger seat. H was a fucking mess. He had been free-basing Charlie for the best part of the day and night and was a complete state, sitting there crying his eyes out and telling me how much of a good mate I was to him, typical free-base bollocks talk.

H became a typical hypocritical wanker that night; only a few weeks earlier he had been checking my arms for track lines and making a point that his views on junkies were that they were nothing but scum and could not be trusted. Now, here was the righteous H sitting in my car at four in the morning, crying like a baby, completely out of his skull. I got him back home just after five, his missus was in bed and I couldn't find any keys in his pockets, so I had to knock her up. No sooner did she open the door, she starts giving me a fucking mouthful, saying it's my entire fault and I should be ashamed of myself and all that bollocks.

I just replied with one question. 'Has he been doing this for long?'

She just looked at me and her face went purple and she was shaking like someone who was about to burst. 'See you, you horrible bastard, don't you dare stand in front of me and claim that you have no idea what this piece of shit,' looking at H lying in the hall-way, 'has been up to, he's been like this for months, you useless sod and its all your doing. He's been seeing and dealing with you, Johnny Mack, for the last four months and each time he does he comes home in this state and with some old tart's perfume all over him, so don't take me for a fucking dumb blond.'

I just looked at her nodding my head in bewilderment and thought the way she was performing, it's just not worth the effort to explain to her that I, this useless sod she thinks I am, had been away off the manor for the last few months. It was fucking obvious that H had been using me as an excuse to his old woman for his late returns. Most of my criminal associates were married and most of them had shagged about and the majority had been caught bang at it, that is except me, I never strayed, I admit that I've been tempted once or twice when some slosh-pot tells me that she wants to suck me dry, who wouldn't, I'm only human and far from perfect, but I was in love with my wife and the way I see it, if you are genuinely in love then why risk losing that special person for a few moments of lust. That was where I was different to my pals; I always told Carol what was going on with my mates, so she would be prepared for when one of their' wives or girlfriends would pull her to one side, especially when I had the night club running they would often say to her that if their old men were at it, then I must be as well. These shit-stirring bitches tried many times to break-up my marriage but they always failed.

I might not be an honest person in some ways but in others I am honest and loyal, not only with my working pals but also with my marriage. They were just jealous of our relationship and wanted to fuck it up because theirs was shit. There was one thing these wives and girlfriends ironically didn't mind though, was their men going out with me, whether it was business or social, because deep down they knew I wasn't at it, fucking hypocrites, and there was a good chance that they knew whilst their old men were out with me they wouldn't be shagging anything else. Now they were all tumbled because H had an old woman with a big fucking mouth and before mid-day my name would be shit in the wives and girl friends fraternity and to be honest I didn't give a fuck what they thought anyway. So I'm standing in the hallway with H flat out on the floor and rent-a-mouth giving me nothing but grief, I just turned and walked away with her effing and blinding behind me. I just stopped at the door and was now starting to get the hump with all the abuse she was dishing out and I said, 'Why don't you just give it a rest? And while I'm at it, if I was married to you I'd have to come home like H every night just to put up with you. I can't see what he sees in you, you're just a fucking Essex tart gone wrong, so do me a favour and fuck off to where you crawled out of and another thing, if you were a geezer talking to me like that I'd have slit your fucking throat, so button it bitch.' Then I went back to my car and turned on my stereo and listened to Mozart; that always helped me calm down and chill. I was left thinking all sorts of things, especially about H, so I made my way back to my in-laws and got a few hours kip so that I could be a bit more with-it and deal with it after I woke up; there's an old saying – sleep on it. That afternoon I got up and made my apologies to my sister-in-law for the performance earlier, then went to work at the mini-cab-firm, just to get away from everyone and to earn a few bob because I was near on skint. About three in the morning I got a call over the radio to pick up a punter from a pub in Deptford High Street, which was well known for lock-ins.

I tapped on the window of the pub in the generally accepted secret code which most lock-in pubs were aware of – Tap-tap----tap-tap, which to those punters inside would indicate a taxi was outside waiting. I sat there in the side turning next to the pub for a few minutes, when the side door opened half way and out pops H. First thought that went through my mind was a repeat performance of last night, but he was normal this time and walked to the car and got in the back and shut the door and said, 'Peckham, driver.'

I just started the car up and headed for Peckham, not saying a word, just looking in the rear view mirror at H in the back, he was just staring out of the side window in a world of his own really, very quiet and paying me no attention. After ten minutes, I'm parked up right outside his house and turned the engine off.

Then H turns to me as I'm viewing him through the rear mirror, and he says, 'Who fucking told you to come here? I only said Peckham, not here,' and with that we both got eye contact in the mirror. 'What the fuck is this, Mack?'

'Feeling better now are we H?' I said with a bit of sarcasm.

'What the fuck are you doing in this piece of shit of a motor?'

'Fucking trying to keep my head down, H, something you should have been doing last night. Anyway, do you want to tell me what the fuck you're up to? You lost a lot of respect from me after what you done last night.'

'I'm sorry, Mack, about last night. I had a few too many, that's all, bro.'

'That's the biggest load of bullshit I've ever heard, H. You were completely off your trolley on free-base mate. Please don't take me for a cunt, H, or I will just walk away from this piece of work, I mean it! The truth or I walk.'

'Okay, okay, Mack, you just sound like my old woman.'

'Your old woman, H, fuck me mate, she laid right into me last night, she's a fucking nightmare, she blames me for everything.' I pointed my finger at him the way when you're being told off by your parents as a kid. 'You've been using me as an excuse for fucking months and to be honest, I need to talk about this tomorrow not tonight because I'm so fucking angry and I know we will end up falling out, so I'll see you later, H.'

He got out of the motor, and then he sticks his head in through the passenger window and says, 'Nice cover, Mack, this mini-cab game.'

'Yeah, you're right there, H. That's four quid for the fare, mate.'

And with that, H throws a score on the seat and tells me he will bell me tomorrow. I knew there and then that H had to make a decision that night, either tell me a load of bollocks or the truth. He knew I was no mug because we had known each other for years and he knew that I would know if he was bullshitting me. I called it a night and went back to my in-laws to get some well earned shut-eye.

'It's that fucking nightmare of a mate of yours on the phone for you, Johnny,' my sister-in-law shouts from the kitchen.

I thought that can only be one geezer and went and got the phone. I said, 'Hello H, what's happening?'

'Meet me at the North London gaff in four hours, Mack.'

'Why over there, H? Can't you make it nearer, mate?'

'Can't do that, Macky-boy, we need to talk, mate.'

'Okay, H, I'll be there in four, see you later.'

This time I went part of the journey by car, leaving it near the Elephant and Castle tube station, which was one of the best tube stations to lose a tail because there were two, inter-linked by underground walk-ways, the Bakerloo and the Northern lines, which were ideal for getting away from anyone, including our boys in blue.

When I arrived at the safe house H let me in and by the state of the place he had been there all day. 'We've got too talk, mate.'

'Fucking right we have too, H.'

'Listen, Mack, I've been doing too much of that crack and it's fucking with my head mate.'

Well what could I say to him? 'Yeah, mate, I know where you're coming from, mate, because I recently just kicked a Crack and Skag habit.' Of course I couldn't say a fucking word, could I, because I had been through the interrogation bit with H already when we first met up again and I couldn't lose face. 'How long has it been going on for, H?'

'About four months, Mack, I've done a bundle on it.'

'Are you using, every day?'

'Near on, Mack, especially over the last two months. I'm doing about eight to ten rocks a day.' I done a quick calculation that a rock can cost between fifteen and twenty quid a throw. H was certainly doing a bundle, near on a fourteen hundred quid a week habit and with that sort of problem, your thinking is none too good and you start making mistakes, and mistakes equals prison or worst.

'H, what's your plan after this bit of work?'

'I've got to get myself straight Mack, maybe go to one of those rehab places or something.'

I said to him, 'Have you tried stopping?'

'Stop? For fuck's sake, Mack, every time I try, I turn into another geezer and go off my head. Only last week I went to my dealer and he was out of stock – well, I was ok for a few hours, then I find myself back at his gaff and put a knife to his throat, demanding him to give me his personal stash. That's what happens when I try and stop.'

I just thought to myself, this is all I need, a fucked up geezer with a lovely bit of work, what should I do? My brain was telling me to fuck right off out of there as quick as possible, but my heart was telling me – you promised your wife and kids that you would be going to the Isle of Wight with enough money to start afresh, not turn up empty handed with fuck all. I know my Carol wouldn't believe me, she would just think it was another load of bollocks to try and stay in Peckham for a bit longer, so I had to make a choice; stay and take a chance and hope all goes well or simply walk away. I decided to stay, justifying that decision with what I had promised Carol because I was the sort of guy who stuck to his word, wasn't I? But the truth was, I was fucking desperate and all the justification in the world could not alter that, so now I was working against everything I had been taught over the years from the elder villains – 'Never work when you're

desperate, son, because you can, and probably will, take silly risks.'
And that's how most of us get caught in one way or another.

Now I had to plan this bit of work very carefully, get my whack,
cover my arse and fuck off into the blue wide yonder, easier said than
done when you realise that you're working with a psycho, a Crack-
head and his yes man, good odds for someone who is desperate for
cash.

'H, have you accounted for any come-backs when this job goes
down mate?'

H just stared at me and said, 'There won't be any come-backs
Mack.'

'H, what about this source of yours that's been giving you all the
info on the other firm that the diplomat has been working with? It's a
dot on the card that when this bit of work goes down the other firm are
not going to be none too pleased about having all their Charlie nicked.
What's his part in this H?'

'Mack, it's all taken care of, no come-backs and my source is as
sound as a pound. Anyway, what's with all the questions?'

'H, I want to carry on living after this, that's why I'm asking all
these questions.'

'Have I ever let you down before, Mack?'

I hesitated for a moment. 'No, H, you have not, but you have
never told me you're a Crack-head either! And we all know what sort
of damage a Crack-head can do, don't we, H?' and with that H jumps
to his feet fucking fuming, fists clenched with a wild-eyed look. 'Did I
hit a sour note, H?' I could see he was trying his hardest not to steam
into me; don't get me wrong when I say that I was a bit weary of H,
because I was. He had a reputation of being an evil bastard when he
had to be and the last thing I needed was him and me rolling around
the floor trying to kill each other. What I wanted from H was for him
to let me take the reins on this bit of work – after all, his own words
were 'you can't trust a junkie, and that's exactly what I told him after
stepping forward and putting my face so close to his that I could smell
his breath. We stayed like that for a minute or so in complete silence

making just eye contact. This was one of the few times in my life that I was scared, but I had to show face and not back down. This is how you gain respect in the criminal world.

H knew he was in the wrong and changed his tone and said to me, 'Mack, you're right mate, I can't function properly while I'm hooked on this shit, so I want your help, for you to take over, not completely, but enough to look after all our interests. Will you agree to that, Mack? Will that make you feel better?'

I said with a slight smile, 'You would make me feel a lot better if you sat back down.'

And with that H starts laughing and says to me, 'I've fucked up, haven't I, Mack?'

'Well, put it this way, H, if it wasn't for my present situation I would have walked the first time you mentioned you're Crack problem and that's the only reason I'm still here.'

H just gave me a nod, after all he knew that he had lost face, and my respect for him was dwindling. I left him at the safe house after we agreed that I would be planning the blag and all he had to do was find out, what date the diplomat would be leaving and returning with the goods. I knew he could obtain that information from his source and Assam. The original deal with Assam was that we were getting the V.A.T. which would be about forty four grand, but with a bit of bartering H managed to round it off to an even fifty, which was acceptable to me, considering I never had a pot in my pocket. The bonus on this one was the Charlie and that had a selling price of twenty-five grand a kilo and if H's source had his sums right, there was a possibility of four or five kilos, cut it could be turned into six or seven kilos, plus whatever else this bent official was bringing into the country, so all in all it could turn into a very nice touch. I got in touch with Billy a few days later and made a meet outside the manor – well to be honest, because it was Billy I took extra precautions and met the nutter in Brighton. We both knew the place like the back of our hands because we used to go there a lot as teenagers in our mod days. We met at a pre-arranged meeting point, and Billy greets me and starts hugging me and trying to stick his tongue down my throat.

'Bill, for fuck's sake, get fucking serious will you!'

Billy gives me this child-like look and says, 'Just glad to see you Mack, that's all you miserable cunt.'

I just had to look at Billy and would think that he had a definite reservation at Broadmoor or Rampton mental institutions, the type of place where they put the criminally insane because without doubt he was psychotic and had got worse over the years and I'm here trying to sort a piece of work out with him. 'Bill, have you spoken to H recently?'

'Yeah, Mack. Spoke to him just after we arranged this meet and he has already let me know that you're sorting most of this work out.'

I said to him, 'Look, mate, what I say goes on this one, do you understand me, Bill?'

'Yeah, I understand Mack. I'm happy with that.'

'Do you know why, Bill?'

'Because you're good at what you do, Macky-boy. You and me have always worked that way, so why all the questions?'

What I was trying to find out from Billy boy was – did he know about H and his slight free-base problem. 'Just making sure you know your place on this one, Bill. The last thing we need is anyone getting hurt because the way it's been worked out, there won't be any come-backs, unless someone gets hurt. You're only there to back H and me up, nothing else, do you get the picture?'

Billy looks me straight in the eye and says, 'Where do you want me?'

I said to him with the same look, 'I want you outside, Bill. Are you happy with that?'

'What do mean outside? I'm never outside, I'm always up the front and I'm not being put anywhere outside, Mack!'

This was what I expected from him. I knew he would react this way – as I already said Billy had to be worked and I already had a plan laid out for him which would involve using a bit of psychology.

'Billy, I'm not asking you to be outside with Chris in the motor,' – on all the work we done together in the past, Chris was always our driver and he was one of the best I'd ever come across, fucking idiot turned down a career in formula racing because he would be away from H. that's why he was called 'H's yes man' – 'Bill, H and I want you in the building, but outside the penthouse door, to make sure we are okay, savvy? You fucking mad bastard.'

'Well! Why didn't you say that in the first place?' He then starts the hugging and laughing routine. I thought to myself, that was easy done and I was now a bit happier that he would not be on the inside with H and me. Then he stops laughing and acting the clown and gives me one of his wild looks and says, 'Tooled-up Mack?'

And I'm thinking, for fuck's sake it's like dealing with a kid and his toys. 'Of course, Billy-boy, tooled-up but only small arms, nothing too heavy, okay?'

'I'm fine with that, Mack, now let's get some fucking grub because I could eat a horse.' Watching Bill eat was a challenge on its own, he ate like a pig, and he could be heard eating a mile away, so I declined the offer by telling him that I had other things to do whilst I was in Brighton. 'Got a bit on the side, then, Mack, have we?' and gives me a wink.

'Yeah, something like that, Bill, I'll be in touch, mate, and don't forget, Bill, keep a low profile mate, okay?'

'Yep, got it, mate, see you soon Macky boy.'

I made my way back to London by coach to Victoria, and then jumped a cab to Peckham via Vauxhall. If I had said to the black-cab driver 'Peckham' he would have given me some old bollocks, 'I only do the City' or some crap like that because black-cab drivers classed Peckham as a no-go area because of its reputation, so I would say 'Vauxhall' then, once he was near the Thames, I would then say, 'Sorry about this, mate, but you'll have to take me on to Peckham, I've had a change of plan.' The fucker couldn't say no because of the Hackney Carriage license laws and that's what Peckham was about, a no-go area and no fucker wanted to go there, and there's me who loved the place and didn't want to leave.

When I got back to my in-laws, I belled Chris and told him to sort a motor out, something a bit nippy, four door, and taken from outside London. He understood what I needed; he was good like that so I had no worries there. So far, so good, I thought. I got Billy outside the penthouse and he's happy. H, will be coming up with the info hopefully soon, and Chris will have a motor by the next day, so I was quite pleased with myself and decided to go back to work mini-cabbing as I was fucking skint by using public transport to organise this bit of work and Carol had been whining on about money and I owed my in-laws for rent and food, so it was back to honest work. After all, I might as well get used to it because that was my plan when I got to the Isle of Wight and you know what? I wasn't really looking forward to it.. The fact was, I fucking hated the thought of honest work, but I just kept telling myself that soon I would be with Carol and the kids, over and over, hoping I'd come round to the idea that it was, slowly but surely sinking in.

About two weeks went by with no contact from H and I was starting to flap a bit because of money, the heap of shit I was driving would be better off in a scrap yard instead of being a taxi. Constant breakdowns and six pints of oil a day were costing me so much that I could have bought something half decent with the dough that I had laid out on it. I just kept thinking that it wouldn't be long before H came back to me with good news so I prayed every morning that this piece of shit of a car would start so I could earn a crust. Some days, I worked 20 hour shifts, a thousand miles in twenty hours most days, and that's why I prayed that she'd start and hold out for another day.

About a week later H bells me to arrange another meet over in North London again. This time I didn't complain, I would've met the fucker in Scotland if need be, because now I was desperate, but I had to ask him if things were sweet.

'Sweet as a nut, Mack. Just get your arse over here pronto.'

This time I got one of the drivers from where I worked who had a pick-up that way to give me a lift, and was dropped off about half a mile from the safe house. I fucking hated driving through North London, let alone walking through it, to me the place was the pits and it had this strange weird smell, something I can't explain really, there are other parts of London where I feel at complete ease. I got to the safe house and before I could even ring the bell, H opens the door.

'Hello, Mack, come into the living room mate, got some good news mate.' He was racing around the room like a whippet and he had eyes like saucers.

'H, you're out of your fucking skull! How the fuck can you sort anything out with me if you're in this fucking condition?'

'What the fuck did I say to you before, Mack?'

'I don't know, H, why don't you fucking remind me?' I said, sarcastically.

'I told you, Mack that I can't get off the shit! And I also told you what I was like when I'm not on it – I've got all the info and I've even got the combination to the front door lock of the penthouse building, so I might be buzzing but I'm working to plan, so really Mack why don't you concentrate on the work instead of me.'

I knew it was pointless arguing with him because he was buzzing and he had done what he had said, so I decided to calm the situation down by asking for a drink.

'Brandy okay, Macky-boy?'

'Yeah, make it a large one,' and as he hands me the drink I noticed that his Rolex is missing from his wrist. 'Where's the kettle, H?'

'In the mender's, mate. Now, let me tell you what's been happening.'

I stopped him in mid flow. 'Mender's, don't take me for a cunt, H, you can't take a bent Rolex into the mender's, they check the serial numbers. You've spunked it away on free-base, haven't you?'

He just gave a sigh and said, 'Yep, but not all on rocks. I had to pay someone off as well. How else do you think that I come across this information? So, yeah, after the pay-off I admit I done some on rocks, fucking satisfied now are we, Mack?' Before I could reply he was off again. 'I wonder about you sometimes, Mack, because you don't miss a trick, does ya? In fact I'm glad you're a villain and not the fucking old bill.'

'How are you going to be on the night, H?'

'Fine, Mack, just fucking fine. Just you worry about the bit of work and not me, I promise I won't fuck things up, okay?'

What choice did I have? I did wonder how he would be on the night, but if I took control of things, hopefully it would work out. I said to him 'Try and balance it out on the night, so you're not spaced out. Anyway, what's been happening?'

'The diplomat is leaving this Friday and will be back Saturday week; also there has been an order for the Charlie.'

I cut in straight away. 'How much Charlie, H?'

'About four to six kilos. I couldn't go too deep; otherwise I might have drawn attention to my source.'

So the way I looked at it was, a minimum of four kilos would bring our whack to hundred fifty grand with the KGs and if there was six kilos that would bring it to two hundred thousand, plus extra if we cut it and there was always that thought of what else we might find.

'What about the night porter, H?'

'Chris and Billy have been watching the place at night, for the last few weeks and the porter, goes regular as clockwork at three o'clock to an all night café around the corner for his breakfast, which is ready and waiting for him, so it's pre-arranged and he's gone for exactly forty-five minutes.'

I said, 'We only need fifteen minutes.'

'I know Mack, not even that. Sounds sweet don't it, no cameras just this old porter geezer and he will be munching into his breakfast when we go in.'

'What about the penthouse door, have you got that sorted?'

'No problem, Mack, it's one of those new swipe cards you use in place of a key. I can open that in five seconds without a sound.'

I knew H was a genius around electrics and if he says he can open that door in five seconds then I believed him and I said, 'So we catch the diplomat in bed?'

H said, 'Exactly, while he's all sleepy and dopey, he won't know what's hit him.'

'H, how sure are you that he will have the stash there and not at his official gaff?'

'Because, Macky-boy, he's got a meet at seven in the morning with the Charlie firm at the penthouse and then he's got a meet with Assam at ten. Do you want to put odds on it?'

'No, it sounds sweet to me. Well done mate.'

'I told you that I would come up trumps Mack.'

'Listen, H, I want you to promise me something and when I mean promise, I mean I want your word and hand-shake on it, that when this is all over, please get yourself sorted, will you do that for our friendship and your kids?' I didn't mention his old woman because I fucking hated her after all the shit she threw at me previously.

H gave me this big grin and came over to me and gave me a hug and said, 'Mack, I give you my word and here's my hand.' We both shook hands and to our fraternity that was it! No going back on your word or hand shake otherwise you would lose face and H had lost more than his fare share. I know he was trying to make amends with me and I also knew that he was trying to win my respect back.

I left H at the safe house and made my way to the Elephant and Castle by the tube and then got the over-head train back to my in-laws. My sister-in-law was there to greet me and told me that I had several calls that day and was given a number to phone, I recognised it as a number Bill used and went out to the public phone box to make the call, it was always much safer to use call boxes.

'Hello? Is that you Macky-boy?'

'Yep, it's me, Bill. What's up mate?'

Bill sounded quite anxious. 'Been fucking let down on the tool for the work.' He was obviously referring to the gun we had ordered from a dealer we used – our own little arsenal of weapons only consisted of two pump action shotguns and two .45 hand pieces and seeing that we were only taking small arms on this one, we did need a third. I said to Bill to try an old friend of ours called Russian George; in fact he came from Romania, so some bright spark called him Russian George and the name stuck.

I told Bill, 'Give him a call and tell him I sent you, okay, Bill?'

'Will do, Mack, and I'll let you know what the score is.'

'Alright, Bill, but remember we only have a short time to get one and if that fails then it will have to be a replica.'

Bill's reaction was spontaneous. 'Fucking toy gun! What type of a cunt do you take me for Mack? I'd rather take the pump than take a fucking toy.'

I was losing patience now with this lunatic. 'That's real fucking shrewd of you, isn't it, Bill? You, walking in a penthouse with a piece that's the length of your arm and if it goes pear-shaped and you use it, you would wake every fucker up within a mile radius and apart from that, you're end up topping someone with that cannon. I have already said we would limit the violence, not start a fucking war! Just do as you're told Bill, for fuck's sake.'

'Calm down, Macky-boy you miserable bastard. I'll sort it with the Russian.'

That was the thing about Billy; he was a loose cannon waiting to go off at any time and I can assure you Billy and a pump action don't mix.

A few days later I was in my local, the Marlborough Head, and there was a message behind the bar for me. The landlord Jim tells me that the Russian wants a word with me ASAP.

'Thanks, Jim,' I said and drank my drink and made my way to where the Russian had a shop with his flat above, not far from the pub. I assumed Billy had fucked things up as usual and George would be none too pleased, so I prepared myself for the worst. This was usual when you left things to Bill.

I belled George from a call box just around the corner from his, to make sure that there would be no-one with him. George was a fence and he would buy anything, so he was always busy – it was always best to bell before you called on him. George answered and directed me to the rear of his shop and met me at the back door.

'Hello, George, what's happening, mate?'

George was a very shrewd geezer and had a very high respect from the criminals he dealt with, so he was a 'Face'. In his individual accent, which sounded like a Russian cockney, he said, 'What-are-you wanting-with-silencer-Mack?'

I said, 'Silencer?

'Yes-Mack-Silencer.'

I told him I was in no need of a silencer, just a .38 or .45 hand piece.

George said, 'You-have-been-given-45, so-why-silencer?'

I could only put this down to fucking Billy, can't even send him on a simple errand without him causing problems. I told George that Billy was to just collect a piece and nothing else. George was a bit anxious and said that if someone uses a silencer, then there could only be one logical reason and that was to top someone and if that was the case he would want a lot more money. I told him that there was no one getting topped and put it down to Billy, as he is a fucking idiot and I tried to front George out with a bull-shit story that Bill sometimes gets carried away with himself.

'I-hope-so-Mack-for-your-sake and-his.' George was now in serious mode and he was making himself understood even with his weird accent.

'George, have you given him a silencer?'

'Of-course-I-have-Mack, he-told-me-that-You-needed-it-and-that-is-the-only-reason-why-he-got-one.'

Now, I had to sort this out fast otherwise George would suss me out and it would be me losing face. 'Look, George, we are talking Billy here and we all know what he's like, sometimes he thinks he is a fucking commando. The fact is, I don't want a silencer and I didn't ask the nutter to get me one, so what I'll do is get it back from him and return it, okay? I'm sorry about this mate and I should have come and seen you myself instead of that fucking idiot.'

George leant over to me and put his huge hands on my shoulders and gave them a tight squeeze. He was in his mid fifties, a very strong and powerful man, not many people fucked with him, but he was a diamond geezer and I had known him for about five years and trusted him completely. Then he says, 'Johnny,' now I knew that I was about to get a talking to, because he only used Johnny when he was really serious and needed to be understood. 'That-Billy, will-get-you-life-Johnny, do-you-understand-what-I-say Johnny? Life-or-minimum-twenty-five-years, John, how-long-you-know-me?' And before I could answer he says, 'Long-time-no?' and I just nodded in agreement. 'Billy-is-bad-man, he-is-stupid-bastard, why-you-work-with-this-stupid-bastard?' I could feel the grip on my shoulders getting firmer. 'Why?' he asked again.

I said quite calmly that I was on a piece of work that belonged to someone else and that someone else wanted Billy in on it, so, I told him, I had no say in the matter.

George completely understood how the underworld worked, so he let go of my shoulders but still maintained eye contact and said, 'Be-very-careful-my-friend-and-return-my-silencer, if-I- hear-that...'

I cut him short by saying, 'Don't worry, George. I'll get it back.'

'Okay-Johnny, quickly, yes?'

I felt like a school boy being told off by the teacher and replied 'Quickly, George.'

'May-your-God-go-with-you-Johnny-Mack-because-I-am-thinking-you-will-need-him-sooner-then-you-think.'

I gave George a bit of an old fashioned look. What a fucking thing to say. In all my dealings with him, he had never said anything like that before. I knew George had Gipsy blood in him, because his parents were executed during the war by the Nazis, for being fucking pikeys of all reasons and he hated Germans, so that was understandable but I was thinking that, being gipsy, perhaps he could read my future and that bothered me.

I left George's place feeling fucking angry about what Billy had done and tried to dismiss George's last comment and got to the phone box to give H a bell. Lucky for me, H picked up the phone and not his old woman, thank fuck, because it was hard for me to be nice to her and I was not in the mood for her whining voice. 'H, we need to meet tonight, mate, because we got a problem.'

'I'm out tonight, Mack, because I got a bit of important business to sort out. Are you cabbing tonight?'

I told him I had no choice because I was skint, so he said I could pick him up at two in the morning from the same pub as before in Deptford and then we could have a chat.

I was at the pub ten minutes early and parked up down the side. I was thinking to myself that I hoped H was not out of his skull because I needed to talk to him straight, because I was worried about Billy. I got out of the car and went to the window and done the usual routine tap-tap on the window and got back in the motor and waited. As each second went by, I was getting more and more wound up. I kept thinking, for fuck's sake, H, get your fucking arse out here! It didn't help knowing he was on the gear and I could imagine him sitting at a table talking bollocks to a few cronies, knowing I was waiting outside. That's how I think when I'm like that; I've got no patience and need answers yesterday.

Bang on time, H comes out the door and gets into the front with me. 'Hello, Mack, what's happening?' I started the car and drove without saying a word for a minute or two, then H broke the silence 'What the fuck's wrong with you Mack and where the fuck are you going?'

'Listen, H,' I said in a dead serious way. 'I'll tell you what's wrong; fucking Billy is what's fucking wrong.'

H got serious as well and said, 'What's the silly cunt gone and done now then, Mack?'

I tried answering calmly and found even that fucking hard. 'The fucker has made me look a complete wanker H.'

'Well, for fuck's sake, Mack, spit it out will you. What is this, a fucking game show or something, where I have to guess the fucking answer? Just tell me what he's done.'

I said, 'I sent him on that errand, to get the other piece from the Russian and he gets a .45, and then he tells the Russian that I also want a silencer!' My voice was rising as I got angrier and angrier. 'What's he playing at, H?'

He leant over and put his arm round me. 'Listen Mack, I told Billy to ask for the silencer.'

I fucking exploded from all the pent-up rage and pulled the car over just outside Surrey Docks tube station. 'Get out! You cunt, get out!' He was seeing a side of me that he hadn't seen in years except when we were working. I'm out of the motor like a bolt of lightning with a twelve inch iron pipe in hand and went round to his side of the car before he had the chance to open his door. I always had to have one of these in the motor, for protection. When you're mini-cabbing it pays to be careful because of the low life scum bags you pick-up in our area, especially at night.

He wound the window down and saw that I was tooled up and he also knew that he was fucked, especially where he was situated in the passenger seat with fuck-all to protect himself.

'Get out, you cunt!' I yelled, 'or I smash this,' and pointed the pipe at his face, 'right into your fucking boat-race, so get out now!'

I could see fear in his face; the eyes always give that away, that's why I admire boxers when they front each other out in the ring just before the fight, it's all about face.

H shouts at me as if to bring me back to sanity. 'Mack, Mack, slow down mate, I can explain, there's a reason for everything and if you just calm down I'll explain. Please, Mack, just get back in the motor and we will sort it, otherwise we'll get nicked here, right outside the fucking tube station! Get back in, Mack, will ya?' That did bring me down a peg or two and I backed off, saying fuck all and taking deep breaths to calm me down. The thing is with me, if I feel someone or something is taking me for a fool, I can sometimes lose control and my mind goes into black-out and there have been a few occasions where I have really hurt someone badly and not even known about it until afterwards. H knew what I could be like, so he was working me. 'Come on, Macky-boy. Get back in.' I stayed like that for a few minutes and then got back into the motor. H went on to tell me that a source of his wanted a silencer for another bit of work in Spain, so when he found out that Billy was to get a piece from the Russian, he also asked him to get a silencer and to say that it was for me because he said that he owed the Russian a few grand for another piece of work and instead of paying George, he had blown it, and George would not have entertained him if he had asked for it himself.

I said, 'You know something, H? That shit you're taking is turning you into a fucking liability. You know George would want more money, because he's not fucking stupid. Now he wants it back! And I have told him he will get it back, H.'

H just shrugged his shoulders and said, 'Too late, Mack, it's gone. Deal's been done, that's what I've been doing tonight.' Now, I am getting angry again when H says, 'Mack, I got a good price for it and we needed some more dough for this job. We're all skint. I know I took a liberty but I didn't think it would come to this, Mack.'

I said, 'What am I meant to say to George, H?'

He just looked at me and said, 'The truth. Tell him that it's for Spain and he will get a good whack by the end of the week, because we'll have had our earner by then and I will pay him off what I owe him plus the silencer.'

I just looked at him and said, 'I can't believe you have just come up with that.' I'm thinking, here I am, talking to a geezer who's under the influence of free-base, telling me this drug fuelled bullshit. 'Alright, H, I'll tell George the truth, mate!' in a real sarcastic manner and then started the car and made our way back to Peckham. Neither of us spoke for the fifteen minute drive back, my brain was in overdrive now, that old feeling of impending doom was coming over me and I felt uncomfortable with the whole situation. I should have fucked off to the Isle of Wight there and then and followed my gut feeling, but I was desperate.

When I dropped H off he just said, 'We're meeting Friday night over North London at eight o'clock mate, for one last meet before the night. Are you okay with that, Mack?'

I said, 'Okay, H, eight it is.' I drove away thinking what the fuck have I got myself into here, nothing goes easy when you're desperate, so I thought I would call it a night and headed back to my in-laws to try and get my head down.

I got a couple of hours' kip, before my in-laws' kids were jumping all over me, because I slept on the put-you-up bed in the front room. This was the usual practice every morning. Don't get me wrong, I love kids, but I had so much shit firing around in my head, that I snapped at them and the obvious happened, tears and crying. Poor little mites had never seen me angry and I must be honest, I frightened them. With that, Les came down the stairs to find out what all the commotion was about.

I told him that I roared at the kids because I was so tired. Les is a blinding geezer and has brought his kids up to respect elders, a bit like the old school way and started having a go at the kids. I told Les it was my fault and not to blame them, so he sent them off into the kitchen for breakfast. Then he turns to me and says, 'What's up, John? You ain't been right since your mate came round here out of his fucking skull.'

I said, 'Listen, Les, I'll be out of your way in a few days and I want to sort you out with a bit of dough before I leave.'

Les, bless him, he tells me he don't charge family. 'You're going to be alright, John?' Les says, to reassure me.

I looked him straight in the eyes and said, 'I hope so, Les, or Carol and the kids will be pretty pissed off with me.' Carol was Les's sister, so he knew what she was like and apart from that I had put her and the kids through hell, what with the drugs, prison, police, so I feared letting them down, and this bit of work I was on kept popping up unwanted surprises all the time.

49

Friday arrived at last, it just seemed to be the slowest week ever; it was always like that before you went working, and you have to mentally work yourself up into this other horrible geezer, a bit like a Jekyll & Hyde character and I began to dislike myself, probably because of the thought of Carol and the kids and the promises I had made to them all. Carol always wanted a normal husband and life and I always promised her that I would change, but as I already mentioned it was sinking in slowly and was starting to speed up, but now the brakes were on. Until this bit of work was out of the way, so I had to stay focused.

Once at the safe house, the rest of the firm were already there having a beer, with three shooters on the coffee table in front of them, and as usual Billy was in his element, picking them up and pointing them at Chris, who was very weary of Bill, because Billy was so unpredictable.

Before a word was said I shouted at Billy, 'Put the tool down! You plank! Don't you realise you got your dabs all over the fucking pieces?'

Billy just smiled with that greasy spotty face of his and he stands up and says, 'Flap, flap, flap, that's all you fucking do, Macky-boy. I'll give 'em a good wipe, okay, mate?'

I roared at Bill, 'Wipe? Wipe, you cunt? You can't even wipe your own arse, you fucking lunatic!' and with that H jumps up and tries to calm the situation down.

'Fuck's sake, boys! We're all here on business, not in the pub, so let's cool it! And sit down!' H was right. What was the point in having a row with a psychotic maniac, so we got down to business.

Everything was in place; we had the tools, ski masks, car and all the info was pucker. The plan was simple; Chris would watch for the diplomat's return, and then once he was back, we would arrive and wait for the porter to go for his breakfast, go straight into the building via the combination and up to the penthouse where H does his stuff with the swipe card lock and we catch the diplomat in bed. So it was agreed what time we would meet and where, now the work was ready to commence. I stayed on after Billy and Chris left to have a quiet chat with H.

He said, 'What's on your mind, Mack?'

I said, 'Where's this come from, H?'

He replied, 'Where's what come from?'

I said, quietly, 'This calmness. You seem to be in control again mate, so, I'll ask you again, H, where's it coming from? Because you've got me slightly worried now.'

'Don't worry, Mack. I went to the quack and he's put me on valium and it's balanced me right out mate. I'm okay, honest!'

The way I saw it was, I'd rather he be this way than the way he was when he turned up at my in-laws, so I left it at that and made my way back to my side of the river.

I spent the rest of that evening with my in-laws and their kids as this was my last night in Peckham and we had a few drinks and a laugh. It was so good to have family, people you can trust, people who don't care what you are (within reason). Les never asked me anything; he knew I was a villain and never mentioned my work, probably because he would have been told to mind his own business, in all honesty. He is a diamond and I love him for that, because when I was fucked-up after doing cold turkey from the free-base and skag, he put me up and helped me back to health and I never forget things like that.

I left early before the kids got up because I hated goodbyes, especially to the kids, and took my motor to a safe place, just in case I needed it in a hurry later that night. I already had my plan, and that was to fuck-off as quickly as I could with my share, and just vanish, telling no-one except family; this was it for me, my second Eldorado. I had one before, but that didn't quite work out, so, in a way, this was like a déjà-vu experience for me.

Chris picked me up that evening at the pre-arranged meet along with Billy. As I got into the back seat, I glanced at Billy – he had what I used to call his working face on, but this time he looked different. He had a habit of letting his tongue hang out when he was anxious and nervous, and his tongue was nearly on the floor.

'Alright, boys?' I said as I shut the door.

'Hello, Mack, you okay?' said Chris.

'Yeah, pucker, mate. I can't wait to get this one out of the way.' I said, just as I was giving Billy a jokey clip around the ear; nothing happened, no response at all. 'Oy! You miserable cunt I'm talking to you!' Chris piped up and said that he'd been like that since he picked him up. We carried on the journey just listening to the radio, not a word said. As I said before, Chris was a yes man with limited opinions, so was very quiet and reserved and I liked him. He was so inoffensive and never over-shot the mark and he knew his place, but he should have stuck with the formula racing team instead of us, so in a way he was a nice geezer but a mug. I sat and looked at the back of Billy's head, wondering what the fuck was going on in that thick skull of his, because I had never known him so quiet and that bothered me. That scary feeling of impending doom was there, that churning gut instinct and when I look back at it now, I wish I had taken more notice of it because it was telling me that something was not kosher.

Chris drove into the drive of H's sister's place. This was to be our base and H was there to greet us.

'Hello, boys, come in. Chris, go and park the motor at the back, not the front, and don't forget to lock it, there's fucking thieving bastards around here.' Chris just laughed at what H had said, probably because we were the worst bunch of them all and H was being a fucking hypocrite. Then, out of the blue, H lunges at Chris and grabs him by the lapels and pulls poor Chris right up to his face and he says to Chris in a threatening way, 'Laugh at me again, Chris, and I'll fucking bury you, got it?'

Poor Chris just said, very nervously, 'Sorry, H, I was only having a laugh.'

'Not today we aren't, Chris. Now, do as I said and fucking move the motor,' and with that Chris just left the house and done as he was told. H had an incredible hold over Chris.

We spent the rest of the evening just talking and playing cards and watching TV, but what was noticed by me was how everyone was asking one another the time even though there were three clocks on the wall and the later it got the worse it got.

This was common among little firms that worked our way, the whole gang would stay together on the day or even the night before, so everyone had an eye on each other all the time. They say there is honour among thieves, but in fact just before a bit of work every thief is only thinking of looking out for himself, so all that honour shit is a complete load of bollocks. The only rule we stuck too was 'No grassing' – if you grassed then you were fucked, you would lose all respect and probably end up dead and your family would be treated the same, even your kids, and if you were very, very lucky and had police protection you might live, but then again you probably wouldn't. Simple rule, really.

It was late in the evening now and Chris had left an hour earlier to position himself outside the diplomat's penthouse and the three of us were now parked-up about a half mile away in a van. H had managed to get his hands on some pucker walkie-talkies, with a ten mile range and Army combat gear with black ski masks. We sat and waited on Chris to give us the okay. Really, when I think back, we would have made an awesome army unit if we had been in the Second World War, we probably would've done every bank from Calais to Berlin and come back as rich men. I can remember asking my Old Man what he done in the war apart from trying to kill Nazis. Seeing he was a quiet man, it would take a few pints and a few whiskies to loosen his tongue and then he would tell me some amazing stories. He told me one that has me in stitches every time I think of it.

The English had just recaptured Belgium and forced the Germans to retreat, so when the British soldiers marched into a small village, the crowds – mainly women – went mad with excitement and thought the Brits were the business and of course my old man takes full advantage of the situation and wastes no time and pulls a bird who owns the local bar-hotel and he's lapping it up for about two weeks, shagging, drinking, and knowing him, more shagging.

After the two week rest, well, probably not in his case, his unit gets orders to advance When their replacements turn up, in amongst the new Company is my Uncle John (my old man's brother) who is two years younger than the old man, but you would think they were twins, so the story goes Uncle John goes into this hotel to get a drink and within minutes he is whisked upstairs by the old man's bird and given a good session. He's thinking to himself, I've had a right result here, until she shouts out 'William!' in a moment of passion. Good old Uncle John was as sharp as a fox and sussed out that she thinks the old man has come back and he's him and had the same as the old man for about the same time and just let her get on with it; what's the chances of that happening, and I bet she never complained, after all she's just had a month of cock. There are probably a few French Mack's out there, especially the way he shagged himself through the war. Another one was when they had captured thousands of German prisoners who had to be searched and guarded, so my old man joins the Red Caps, only temporary of course, and robbed every German he searched and sent it all home to his mum. He said he got his own back on the Krauts for blowing up his mum's house in an air raid and I suppose he took it personally; well let's put it this way, they paid for his mum's house tenfold.

'This is Tango Delta receiving, over?' Chris said over the walkie-talkie. This made H jump a bit as he had been very quiet and he dropped the walkie-talkie on the floor of the van. I put it down to the valium. He fumbled on the floor of the van looking for it – it was pitch black inside. Anyway Billy sparks his lighter just enough for H to retrieve it and presses the talk button. 'This is Delta receiving loud and clear, what's your situation? Over.'

Chris replied, 'This is Tango, package arrived, lights on over.'

'Roger that, Tango, let me know when all is in blackout, over and out,' and so we waited, for the diplomat to go to bed and the porter to go for his breakfast. What Chris had said over the walkie-talkie was that the diplomat had turned up alone, with a bag, apart from his suitcase, and we all knew the bag was the prize.

It was ten to three in the morning when H came to life after being silent for ages and says to Billy, 'You sorted Bill?' Bill just grunted then H says, 'You, Mack?'

I said, 'Sorted, H. Roll on three o'clock.'

H came right out with it and says, 'It's not three o'clock we have to think about, it's when the fucking diplomat goes to bed.' H was dead right, we needed him in bed, not still up; the last thing we needed was to have to steam in there. For all we knew he may have a panic button straight through to the Old Bill – after all he was a V.I.P.

'This is Tango, over?'

H grabs the walkie-talkie and says, 'Loud and clear, over?'

'Blackout, repeat blackout.'

H answered instantly. 'Roger that, Tango. Go to position two, and await further instruction. Over and out.'

Position two was where Chris would wait for us once we had finished the work. H says to me, 'Mack, how long do you think it'll take him to nod off?'

I told H that he must be knackered after his flight.

'Yeah, he must be. Let's give him till twenty past, and then we go in. Okay, boys?'

Then, from the back of the van Billy opens his mouth at last, after spending most of the day zombie-like. 'What if he's had some Charlie and is wide awake and is at this moment cutting the coke, eh? Thought of that, have ya?'

H just growled at Billy, 'Shut the fuck up, Bill, because you talk complete and utter bollocks! What's he doing, Bill? Cutting it in the fucking dark?' Bill went to say something when H starts the van up and says, 'Fuck it. Let's do it now.'

I said to H, 'We're only a couple of minutes early. Let's do it,' rubbing my gloved hands together in anticipation of my luck changing and the adrenalin started to rush in. It's the best rush ever, there's not a drug that can match it and I should know that better than anyone.

H drove within the speed limit as there was hardly anyone about at that time of morning except the old bill and milkmen. He drove to a cul-de-sac at the side of the penthouse apartments; it was a perfect location as it was nice and dark and we were parked right next to the apartment's side garden gate with plenty of bushes for cover. I felt good about that because wearing the army kit we could get noticed in the area we were in. The only reasons for wearing this type of kit is to frighten your victim, you can burn it after the work was done to destroy any forensic evidence, plus it was near on impossible to trace as it was all army surplus, it wasn't meant to be worn in the street. H jumped into the back with me and Billy and grabbed his little bag of tricks and we all got out of the side door nice and quietly and made our way to the entrance of the garden gate. Once inside the grounds, we stuck to the shadows and bushes so as not to be seen from the high street and got within a few metres of the main doors which had the combination box next to them. Now, if we were to go to the main door with all this combat gear on we could have been seen from the street, so H pulls a rain coat from his pocket and puts on a flat hat (like the porter's hat), puts them on and leaves Billy and me behind these bushes and goes straight to the doors and punches in the combination. Straight away the door buzzes and the door swings open; without a word being said H is instantly inside and Billy and I are on his heels.

Once we'd taken care of the telephone at the porter's desk by pulling the wires out of the socket, we dimmed the lights in the foyer as we were still visible from outside and made our way up the shag piled carpeted stairway to the floor where our V.I.P. was situated, walking very quietly H takes off his rain coat and hat just leaving his mask rolled up around his forehead, I was sweating now, the heat with this kit on made me feel uncomfortable. Billy just looked like he stepped out of a shower because he was dripping and his hygiene was none too good.

H pulled out this simple household device which was powered by batteries and he had added two pieces of copper wire to it. He said to me, 'Ready, Mack?'

'Ready H,' as I pulled out my piece in readiness, as did Billy.

H went up to the door, with me behind him, but Billy stayed a few metres away in a darkened alcove just outside the apartment to watch our backs. H proceeded to turn on his device and there was a blue spark as he swiped the slot where the card key would be used. 'Click' and the door opened as H stepped inside he pulled out his piece in readiness. I was amazed how easy it was for H to open this hi-tech security door in seconds; he was a genius with electrics. That's how H gained his respect in the criminal world, by being brought in on some serious pieces of work that required his expertise. Once inside we waited for a few moments for our eyes to adjust to the dark and stayed motionless for a minute to make sure we could not hear anybody moving about. I made my way down the windowless passage by feeling the walls in almost total darkness apart from a thin line of light coming from under the main front door to where the main living room was, in the hope that the diplomat might have left his bag out, but it was nowhere to be seen. I then came back to where H was standing, just inside the main doorway and gave him the 'no bag to be seen' nod, so it was now onto the bedroom where our friend should be asleep. I opened the door very, very, slowly – a lot of doors squeak – I got it half way open and slid inside. It was pitch black and I could barely see in front of me, then I could feel H right behind me and he turned on a pen light. A very dull light lit part of the room, enough for us to see but not bright enough to arouse the shape that was beginning to form in front of us, as my eyes began to focus on the bed.

Our faces were now completely covered apart from the eye slits and, guns in hand; we crept quietly round the bedroom looking for the bag. The only sound you could hear was the diplomat's heavy breathing but the fucking bag was not in sight, and we both knew what that meant. This part of the work had already been discussed and planned; if we could not get the bag without waking him, then it would be obvious that it would probably be in the safe, so we had a plan ready. H went to the bedside lamp and I went to the other side of the bed just as H turned the bedside light on. 'Crack' went the butt of my piece to the side of the geezer's head, just between the ear and lower jaw, enough to stun him, but not knock him out, as we needed him conscious so he would give us the location and combination to the safe. The whack to his head had just had the right effect, complete shock! H grabbed his flailing arms and I put a pillow over his face to restrict his breathing and panic him just enough that he would quickly realise that he had no control over his situation and was powerless. I took the pressure off and raised the pillow slightly pushing the gun under. I told him that if he carried on struggling I'd blow his fucking head off! But even doing that didn't stop him, so I put the pressure back on the pillow as he was still struggling, then H hit him with the butt of his piece in the kidney area, which totally fucked him. I released the pillow so he could get some air and at the same time I rammed the barrel of my gun into his mouth knocking some of his teeth out as it was rammed in with force. I took the pillow away, H was still holding his arms and there was claret everywhere. With the gun still in his mouth I sat astride him and grabbing at his hair, I turned his head round to face me

'I don't want to hurt you, I want you to do exactly as you're told, do you understand what I'm saying to you?' The diplomat blinked his eyes and tried to nod. I could see the fear in his eyes; he was scared shitless which was exactly how we wanted him, totally under our control and not give him time to think. I suppose it was a form of psychology. I then dragged him off the bed by his hair onto all fours. H kicked him in the bollocks from behind. I told H to back off because the diplomat was ready to co-operate, and then calmly, almost friendly, said to the diplomat, 'You are going to, aren't you, my friend?' He nodded again. I said, 'You are going to behave yourself? And when you do, I'll take this gun out of your mouth, okay?' This time, his nod of compliance was more eager so I took the gun out of his mouth very slowly and kept it pointed two inches from his forehead, still holding his hair with my other hand. The claret was pissing out of his mouth and it was going everywhere; I could see he was choking and the last thing we wanted was the geezer to die on us. So I turned him over so he was now sitting upright on the floor.

I knelt astride his legs and sat on his knees, and leant over so that we were almost facing each other, I took the gun away from his head, but still holding his hair tightly I said to him in the same calm, almost friendly voice, 'Do you know why we're here?' He just stared at me.

H said to me in a fast, angry, don't give a fuck tone, 'We're just wasting our time here. Let's just waste this piece of shit. He's taking us both for mugs.' This was our play-acting part, to scare the shit out of the fucker.

The diplomat was looking shitless and trembling with fear as he answered, 'I don't know why you are here.'

I said to him again in the same clear slow calming way, 'Are you willing to listen to what I have to tell you and are you willing to give me the right answers?' I then paused for a few moments then said 'Because if you don't, you will have no second chances.'

There was a short silence. Then H walked slowly behind the diplomat and the geezer's eyes followed him round, full of fear. He tried to turn his head just as H went out of his sight, but I still had hold of his hair and I yanked his head back to face me and at the same time I tapped him on the forehead with the barrel of the piece saying, 'Pay attention to me, not him.' H put the gun barrel to the back of his head and the geezer started to panic and tried to get up because he now thinks he's about to be topped. I said to him, 'Are you fucking deaf? Did I or did I not tell you that there was not to be any second chances?' the diplomat nodded yes in agreement. I said in a slow, methodical tone, 'Now, I know you're an intelligent man so I don't think you want me to repeat the question? Do you understand the question I've put to you already?'

He groaned a yes.

I repeated the question. 'Do you know why we're here?'

He said, 'Yes.'

I said, 'Well?'

He paused; H cocked his gun and pushed the barrel even harder into the back of his head. 'I can pay it back! I can pay it back!' the diplomat said.

I said, 'Pay what back?'

He said, 'You're here for the Charlie, right?'

I said, 'You're half right and half wrong; there are two reasons why we're here. I'm going to ask you these two questions only once, do you understand what I'm saying to you?' He nodded. I said, 'The first is, you have upset the wrong people and they want their money back, can you pay that?'

He said, 'Is it the Charlie you want?'

I said, 'Wrong answer,' and gave H the nod. H whacked him round the back of the head with the butt of his piece. I let go of his hair and he slumped to the floor then I said quite calmly to H, 'Shoot the cunt.' This was still our play-act, we did not want the diplomat to know exactly why we were there, we wanted him to tell us, it saves a lot of time and pain.

H said, 'Pleasure,' and, walked around to the side of him, stood right above him and pointed the .45 straight at him and cocked it. This time he really thought he was going to get it and then he hurriedly pointed to a full-sized bookcase, the type that fits from floor to ceiling. He was mumbling and groaning as he pointed his trembling finger. Then H came out with a classic, totally ad-lib and said, 'Do we look like fucking librarians?'

But the diplomat just kept mumbling in his native tongue and pointing at the bookcase. We realised this must be where the safe was and I asked him, 'What part of it am I looking for?'

He started to crawl towards it and H backed off to let him show us where he was pointing. On the centre shelf was a row of what looked like leather clad books. I pointed at this shelf. 'So what's this?' I said.

The diplomat said, 'It's the safe.'

I said, 'Are you going to open it?'

He readily agreed, but when he tried to get to his feet he couldn't get his balance where he'd been clumped so much. H grabbed him by the arm to steady him and the geezer went to the shelf above the one he'd pointed at and pulled on one book which released the catch on the lower shelf, which sprang ajar a couple of inches. H pulled the whole shelf open which revealed the safe, which was a Chubb combination. H told the diplomat to open it.

I said to H, 'Hang on, be careful, because these hidden safes have got a delayed timer,' and I looked at the diplomat and asked him where the switch was. He told me to push the book he had pulled out back in. As the book went back into place a green light started flashing in the right hand corner. Now green to me was always a good colour, but H, just saw the flashing light and stuck the gun to the geezer's head.

The diplomat said, 'It's okay, it's okay.'

I said to H, 'He's right.'

H said to the diplomat, 'Just fucking open it.'

He stepped forward and dialed the combination in and opened the safe. I grabbed hold of him by his hair again and dragged him back to the bed and told him to lay face down on it. H pulled the ropes out from his bag of tricks and he tied the diplomat up with his legs and arms together behind his back and then gagged him. I went to the safe and pulled open the door and there was 'the bag', my Eldorado. H came over to me after he had performed his bondage skills; I'd already pulled the bag out of the safe. This particular bag had a security seal and from experience these bags contain certain gadgets that can activate and destroy the contents for security purposes, bearing in mind that diplomatic bags are only designed for carrying Government official paperwork, not cocaine and Krugerands! This one was bulging and far too heavy just to have paperwork inside.

I took the bag over to the diplomat and I knelt down alongside the bed, his eyes fixed on mine as I told him that I'm about to ask him a very, very important question and I wanted the right answer. 'Is there anything you want to tell me about this bag before I cut this fucker open?' He nodded yes and I leant over and removed the gag. 'Tell me,' I said.

He said, 'Look under my pyjama top.' To do this I had to roll him onto his side and I ripped open the front of his top, buttons were flying everywhere, and he was wearing a thick gold chain with a key attached, not the normal type of Yale single sided grooved key but a double sided slim grooved one, which I'd only come across once before, so I knew from experience that they could be used anti-clockwise or clockwise. Keys like this are designed so that if the key was turned the wrong way it could activate the security device and destroy the contents.

I said to the diplomat, 'What way do I operate the key?'

He looked at me as if he didn't know what I was talking about,

'Left or right?' I said.

'Right,' he said.

I said 'Are you sure?' He nodded and I took the chain from round his neck and put the key into the lock right in front of his face. This time I asked him again, 'Are you *absolutely* sure?'

He said, anxiously 'Turn it right, turn it RIGHT!' I turned it once and went to open the bag and he shouted, 'No, no, now turn it the other way,' which I did and I heard a click as it unlocked and a hissing sound as the pressurized security device deactivated as the bag was opened.

H came over to me as I opened the bag and started emptying the contents out onto the floor. He said excitedly, 'Is it there, is it there?'

I said, 'No, but there's other stuff here, a bag of coins and four bags of powder.' Obviously we knew that it was cocaine, but didn't let on to the diplomat that we were expecting that. I said to the diplomat, 'What are these coins in here? And where's the fucking money?'

He said, 'The coins are the money.'

All this was part of the play-act, so I said, acting a bit thick, 'Are you trying to fucking tell me that these things are gold?'

He said, 'Yes.'

I asked him, 'What are they and what are they worth?'

He told me, 'They're kugarands and the price depends on the current exchange rate.'

I said, 'Don't get fucking technical with me, you prick. How much money are we actually talking here?'

He said, 'Two hundred and fifty thousand, sterling.'

I picked up one of the four bags of powder and said, 'Is this the Charlie?'

'Yes,' he said. 'That's what you've come for, isn't it?'

I said, 'No, we come for the money you ripped off from the people we work for.' He looked confused and edgy. I said, 'What purity is this Charlie?'

'Ninety percent high grade Peruvian flake.' I asked him where the rest was and he told us that it was a shipment of 4 kilos only. I was getting impatient. 'I'm not talking about this shipment. Where's the fucking rest?'

'But that's it, that's all of it,' he said.

I said, 'Wrong answer,' and hit him on the bridge of his nose with the butt of the piece, which busted his nose, and his claret splattered everywhere. I said, 'The stuff you've been skimming, you fucking dirty scum bag. We know you've been cutting the gear ever since you've been given the orders for these shipments and two hundred and fifty grand is not enough to cover the stuff you've taken.'

His eyes were wide open, almost like saucers; He started sobbing as he realised why we were there. He thought that he'd been clever enough when replacing the Charlie he'd been taking out with equal the amount of some other stuff, which was probably Novocain, which dentists use to numb your mouth. So our play-acting had the desired effect we wanted. He never had a clue we were there for the coins; it was obvious to him that he had been rumbled over the cocaine and was probably thinking that we were there to top him unless he could come up with a plan to pacify us, and the only way to keep us sweet would be a large amount of money. He went on to tell us that he could lay his hands on £50,000, but not that day. H looked at me and I gave him the wink, which meant we would play along with him and pretend to give him a chance by allowing him to convince us that all would be ok by the next day.

'Okay, you maggot,' I said with disgust, looking at this ridiculous piece of shit tied up like a stuffed turkey. We'll give you until four o'clock tomorrow afternoon to come up with the other fifty grand and another twenty five to stop my friend here putting a bullet in your head, because you know that's why we are here.' His face went purple and his eyes rolled as he sweated like a pig. I looked across at H and made certain hand movements as if doing sign language which told H that we might have gone too far with the play-acting. After all we got what we came for and he thinks we were here to top him, for his sticky fingers with the coke, so I decided to calm the situation down which H gave a nod of approval. I told the diplomat that he was a very lucky man, because tonight he was going to live, and that we were taking the Charlie and coins and he was to meet up with us the next day with the money.

The colour on his face changed back to a paler shade of grey instead of the purple and his breathing became more relaxed; we knew we had him thinking that he had a reprieve from his own death sentence. We also knew that this fat pig would fuck off as soon as we had left, as he was not about to part with 75k of his own money, let alone take his chances with the other firm, it wasn't that hard to predict.

He was agreeing with everything we were saying to him and this was his own way of reverse play-acting, but this was to save his own greedy life. We never had any intentions of whacking the scummy bastard after all, he was definitely not going to be there, when the Charlie firm turns up and Assam's cousin would not have a clue that the whole thing was a brilliant scam to fuck him over, absolutely perfect for an Oscar each, or that is how I thought it was meant to turn out. But there were other plans in the offing that H and Billy had designed for this diplomat of which I had no knowledge at all.

I gave the nod to H to put the contents of the diplomatic pouch into his magic bag of tricks and he quickly started to pick-up the coke and coins off the floor while I started to untie the scum bag, He kept patronising me with words like, 'Don't worry my friend, I will not let you down,' All bullshit really.

It was exactly what I expected from him as I had been in this type of situation many times and us humans act rather alike when faced with two armed geezers, or in his case would-be assassins, so we were just going along with him as we had got our prize now and it was time to leave. Looking over at H, who by this time had collected all the gear up and had the bag over his shoulder waiting to leave, I left the geezer's arms tied to the bed and broke the telephone by yanking it out of the wall.

As I was about to leave, I knelt down and whispered in his ear, 'Remember we have given you a chance tonight, don't you try and fuck us over, okay? Because there'll be someone watching your every move till we meet tomorrow and that will be at the gate of Platform One, Victoria Station at four o'clock, am I understood yes?'

'Yes,' he replied.

The way I had left him tied, I reckoned from experience that it would take him about 20 minutes to untie himself and by then we would be long gone with our prize. As we were leaving, H was in front of me, with me a few metres behind, as I came out of the front door onto the landing. I noticed H whispering to Billy who had been outside watching our backs. I closed the front door quietly and watched H going down the stairs in a floating but fast pace and as I passed Billy I stopped to ask him how long we had before the night porter was due.

Billy said, 'Fifteen minutes, Macky boy. Now go and I'll watch your back.'

'Okay, Bill, come out in two minutes okay?'

'Sorted Mack, in two, now go.' He was rushing me and that was not like Billy; my gut instinct came into play and as I got to the top of the stairs I heard a metal to metal screwing sound, a sound which I had heard a few times before in my line of work and, let's put it this way, maybe in a few gangster films as well. As I turned to look back at Billy, he was at the front door of the diplomat's with the magic zapper that H had used to gain entry. In a flash of clarity, I just knew what was about to happen as Billy's arse vanished inside the apartment – the screwing sound that I had heard was a silencer being attached to a piece and seeing Billy had just recently purchased one on my behalf from the Russian, which H had said had been bought for a bit of work in Spain, it didn't take two and two to work out what was going to happen, my gut had been right all along.

I stopped in my tracks and turned and ran back towards the door going after Billy and as I got inside the passage I slowed down and crept into the bedroom, just as Billy got to the bed where the diplomat was trying to free himself from the ropes, I saw Billy frantically trying to screw the silencer on to the barrel of the gun as he was standing over the geezer. I knew what was about to happen and pulled my piece out as I crept up on Billy and as I reached him, I leveled the gun at the back of Bill's head and shouted, 'No, Bill! Drop the fucking piece, you crazy cunt' Billy didn't turn to face me and still had one hand on his piece, and the other on the silencer probably because it had not been screwed tight enough to fire yet. I said again, 'Drop it, you cunt, or I'll drop you right now. I mean it Bill! I'll blow your fucking head off!' Billy, as I said, was a psychotic maniac and loved to hurt people, even if they were complying.

Bill turned his head to look at me as I cocked my piece. 'Macky boy, he's got to go mate, it's as simple as that; it's been arranged from the powers above, Mack, so fuck off! Or fucking shoot me!'

The diplomat was frozen with fear and had pissed himself. Just as I was about to say something, I felt a terrific blow to the back of my head and my piece went flying across the room and I fell head on into Billy, who was now on top of the tied geezer. I was dazed and confused as I turned to see who had clumped me and there was H standing right above me with his gun pointing at me. They say your whole life flashes in front of your eyes when you think you're about to die. Believe me, it does. Even though I was concussed, I was still conscious and I felt real fear now – here I was, on top of Billy and the diplomat with H pointing his gun straight at my head. I was unable to talk because I was in shock and fucked and the look on H's face was something I had never seen before, a real focused, mental agitated look. I was so sure he was about to shoot me, that I made a grab for Bill's gun, which meant turning my back on H.

The first thing I felt was someone standing on me because I had come to, face down on the floor. The diplomat had freed himself and was trying to climb over me. I managed to get myself to my feet and was leaning up against the wall as the diplomat was rushing around the room grabbing his clothes from the floor.

I now knew H had whacked me again with his piece, only this time he had knocked me spark out. I made my way to the bathroom and spewed my guts up down the toilet and my head was pounding, with claret running down my back from the head wounds that H had inflicted on me. I grabbed some tissue to soak the blood up and went into the front room where the diplomat was hurriedly putting documents that we had emptied from the diplomatic pouch into a leather holdall.

I grabbed him and said, 'How long was I out for?'

'About five minutes,' he told me. He must have wondered what the fuck was going on. I was still trying to get my head together, I asked him what had happened and he told me that the crazy one (Billy) had saved my life because the big guy wanted to shoot us both; if it wasn't for Billy threatening H with his own gun, then we would have been both dead. He also said that they were arguing over some plan that they worked out and were blaming each other for the fuck up and it ended with a Mexican stand-off, with each of them pointing their guns at each other until they were disturbed by a noise downstairs which panicked them and ran out of the apartment with the gear leaving me unconscious on top of the diplomat, who was by now trying to untie himself.

It was now clearer to me what had happened. Billy and H had agreed to top the diplomat, because a contract had been put on his head over his dodgy coke deals. H and Bill obviously knew I would have nothing to do with a hit, that's why the silencer was bought and if I had not heard the screwing sound as Billy tried to attach it to the piece, then I would have been out of the building and none the wiser and the geezer would have been brown bread and I could have ended up being wanted for murder. I wouldn't have known anything until the next day at least, as news of a diplomat getting whacked would have made the TV and tabloids.

I knew now that the shit was about to hit the fan and the old survival instincts which I had been taught over the years kicked into touch. I had to get out of here real quick; there was no chance of Chris being outside because he must have been in the know about what was going down.

The diplomat was just about to scramble out of the door, when I grabbed him by his shirt collar and pulled him back roughly. I said, 'Give me your wallet.' He became hesitant and instantly I head butted him square on the bridge of his already busted nose – he just screamed in agony and fell to the floor. I had no time for arguing and just put my hand into his jacket and pulled his wallet out and fled the room on to the foyer stairs. I was panicking a bit because the porter must have been due back at any moment and I didn't need any bother from an old war hero, as they love to have a go. Lucky enough he was still not back at the building and I fled through the doors out into the grounds, making my way on to the street. Now, I knew London like the back of my hand and made a decision to make my way to an all night cafe just a few streets away, mostly frequented by taxi drivers, pimps and prostitutes. As I hurriedly half ran and half walked to my destination, my thinking was becoming clearer and now it was dawning on me that I was now in big trouble and had to get out of the manor real sharpish.

As I approached the cafe I could see that it was busy, with all the taxis and the pimps' BMWs outside so I slowed my pace so as not to draw attention to myself and pulled my woollen mask out of my pocket and, putting it on my head rolled it up to look like a bobble hat. This would hide the gash on my head, courtesy of my good pal H.

As I entered the cafe, a waft aroma of smoke, bacon and stale steam came from the place, a real warm and inviting aroma. I looked at a taxi driver who was just coming away from the counter having just paid his bill. I approached him and asked him if he was working. He looked me up and down and said, 'Where to?'

I replied 'Just down the road mate, a nice quick one for you!' He just gave me a nod and a grunt and we both left the cafe and got into his taxi, then I told him exactly where I wanted to go. While we were on our way I thanked God for giving me a sixth sense because that gift had made me leave my motor parked up out of the way, for that 'just in case' sort of problem us criminals would come across from time to time. I checked the diplomat's wallet and found about forty quid and a few credit cards. I had a quick look at the names on them and knew they were no good to me because the fucking name was foreign and no use to me at all. Once we got to my destination, I quickly weighed off the driver and got in my car once he drove off, as I put the key in the ignition, I prayed she would start, because it had an old battery and the temperature at that time was at least minus two. She fired up after a few turns and I sighed with relief making my way back to home ground in South London, not really knowing where the fuck I was going or doing. As I got to Vauxhall Bridge my mind was on H and Billy and at what had just kicked off. I knew it would be pointless trying to go after them as they would have gone to ground, not even fucking Lassie could have found them. Anyway, I knew Russian George would get wind of what had happened and the shit would without doubt hit the fan, so I wanted out now – fast. I had just about had enough of this shit life existence and the thought of Carol and the kids waiting for me was enough to make up my mind and get the fuck out of London away from all this madness, with or without my Eldorado. But first I had to try and get some money real quick, so I decided to head for Deptford to a black geezer called Dexter, who I knew would buy the dodgy credit cards from me. The Peypes Estate was my destination and it was early morning with only the old bill, and milkman out and about, and of course mini cabs. Since I had been using my motor for mini-cabbing, I had my taxi radio aerial on the roof and it looked quite distinctive so generally the old bill would leave you alone providing you had a bit of road tax on the windscreen. I took the lift to the fourth floor of the block and hammered on the door of Dexter. He was a picture when he opened the door. He looked like he had just been given electric shock therapy because his hair looked like it had been frazzled where he had been sleeping on it. He was none too pleased with me, but business is business and being criminals we would often work unsocial hours, so he knew the score. There was an unofficial price for stolen credit cards, so there was no hassling and just a little chat and I was quickly weighed off. I left with two hundred quid, a pittance compared to what I thought I was going to come back with, but the way I looked at it, I was lucky to be alive and being skint was only a minor setback for me. I would have to just treat it as one of those unexpected things that happen, it went with my chosen occupation. The truth was staring me in the face though; I fucked up big time and was lucky to still be breathing, it was as simple as that, so I felt sort of grateful for the amount I received from Dexter. I was now ready to leave, all my worldly belongings fitted into the boot of the car and all there was between the family I loved and me was ninety miles of road and three miles of water.

Carol had told me that she and the kids had been allocated a beautiful white cottage near the coast from the Local Council, then just to get my attention a little bit more she told me it had red roses around the front door, which she knew would describe our idealistic dream home which we would often fantasies about, especially when we were down on our luck and skint. It was our way of making those shit times seem not so bad and it even gave us hope for the future, even though it was just projected dreaming. I believed every word she told me, it was her cunning plan to get me away from the life I was living in South London. I kept that cottage dream locked away in the back of my mind; that dream kept me going many a dark night when I would be in some dingy police cell or prison. So I was considering myself very lucky now; I might not have had the result I expected from the bit of work that evening and seeing I had been double crossed and nearly shot by my so-called best mate, I still had something to fall back on, which was the chance of being with my family in our dream cottage by the sea and that for me, was the best result a man could ask for.

I made my way to Clapham common to pick up the A3 and headed for Portsmouth. My mind was racing now as reality set in – I badly wanted payback on H. After all I'm sad to say he broke our bonded handshake and turned into a rat, but that's what was happening at that time with some of the best criminal talent in South London's underworld and it was all down to fucking drugs! I should know, I had already been there, but had the good sense to get out of that hell before I fucked-up and broke my bonded word to those I worked with. It would have been only a matter of time if I stayed on the gear, so I considered myself very lucky and fucking stupid for letting this work go pear-shaped. It had all the makings and warning signs of a complete disaster yet I let the shit hit the fan, all because I became desperate. When I think about it now, I know that piece of work was never meant to be, yet, at the time, greed and desperation were my masters and once they take hold and set in, you become a liability and work against your own will. H would have been aware that the Russian would be after him over the silencer and I'm sure the Charlie dealers would probably have wanted a very quick word with him and Billy, so I decided to let it go and let nature run its course and try to restart my life, with a new home, new location, and a new life as a normal person. The thought seemed alien to me and to be honest a bit scary, only now, I had no choice, I had burnt all my bridges between that world and this new coming one. Well, that's what was going through my mind at that time.

At Petersfield, the engine went bang with clouds of smoke coming from under the bonnet. I just looked up at the sky and said, 'Nice one, what's next God?' The engine had seized as it had started to snow, I was knackered from lack of sleep and my poor head was killing me and on top of that, I was fucking skint – a good way to start a new life, well planned. I started to walk around Petersfield town looking for another form of transport and after a while I came across a motor bike parked up in a car park. I wasn't a biker fan and confess that the only things that I had ridden of that type were push bikes and scooters but to me it was a form of transport and they were easy to steal. The owner had kindly left his helmet, so with a quick 'twist and snap' of the steering lock, I was in business and off I went with my worldly belongings now fitted into a holdall.

By now the snow was coming down heavy and I didn't have any waterproofs so by the time I had got to Portsmouth my clothing was frozen and I'm sure I had hyperthermia. I managed to warm up a bit on the ferry over to Fishbourne; I knew roughly where to go when I arrived on the Island and made my way to a place called East Cowes where Carol and the kids were waiting for me at our warm dream cottage by the sea with red roses round the door.

# II

At first Carol and I blossomed in this environment and we were both very happy – we had started to live like a family for the first time. I felt really good health wise; after all I had started to walk on average ten miles a day, no drugs, no booze, and early nights with plenty of loving and regular meals made the first few weeks in our new surroundings more like an adventure holiday for all of us. We would all go on mega hikes along the coast line, do fishing and beach combing, it was all new to the kids and they loved it. I was now feeling alive and very grateful for having such a wonderful caring wife and family, whereas before I sometimes took them for granted. But now I was spending all my time with them and I started to actually get to know them as a dad and husband and not the geezer who just flitted in and out of their lives. I suppose I had been a very selfish person when living in London – I was taught that I had to be, because to survive on the streets you had to have a reputation or belong to a credible gang, so it was all a front when I was out on the streets, the way I would walk, talk, look, it was all bollocks and Oscars. What I never learnt to do was switch off once I arrived home from working the streets; I brought my work home with me and my family lived it. They had seen things that other kids would never come across in a million Sundays. Carol and I educated them to be streetwise yet not get involved in the criminal fraternity, I just wanted my children to grow up and be everything I was not and it was this responsible thinking that kept me going. I only ever wanted the best for my wife and kids and I convinced myself that it was my purpose in life to provide for them in the best way I knew. It all sounds justified, but the truth was, I was a criminal and I liked being one and I liked the buzz the life brought. The only trouble was, I wasn't a very successful one.

Our money had run out after the first few weeks and we had been living on government hand-outs. We had been in this situation many times before, so we knew how to live cheap, but not for this long and I was getting fucking sick of soup and mash potatoes and now wanted some decent grub, but we had no money. I had promised Carol that I would stay straight, so a bit of thievery was out of the question and the only option was to get a job. The thought made me cringe, but I had promised Carol that I would get a job and lead a normal life – it all sounded good at the time I was making all these promises but now it was time to cough up and carry them out.

I was offered a job interview in a local boatyard as a paint sprayer. I had done a bit over the years, especially when we would steal cars to order then re-spray them, change the plates, add a new log book then sell them on as legal, so I thought I'll blag it as there can't be much difference between a boat and a car. At the boatyard I was led into a plush office and behind the desk was this yachtie-cum-hooray Henry geezer. He came from behind the desk to greet me and I nearly burst out laughing because he was dressed only in his y-fronts and a thick sailor's polo neck jumper. He explained that he had just returned from sailing, but I reckon he was having a quick wank before I went in – anyway, he was going on about this special paint that was to be used on this newly designed prototype racing yacht and how expensive it was and how you had to be a top quality sprayer to use it. I just nodded, hummed and hahed and just agreed with everything he was saying. But the truth was, I knew a lot less than him.

From under his desk he produced a sample piece of painted board which looked like coloured glass and then handed it to me and says, 'Well Mr. Andrews,' (my new alias) 'can you spray to that standard?'

'Yeah, no problem,' I replied instantly with a very confident smile. He seemed to pick up on it and smiled back at me and leant over the desk and shook my hand and briefly explained that only two people in the UK had the skill and ability to use this paint, and then he explained that he was willing to give me a trail period and offered me the job. To be honest I wasn't that chuffed at getting the job. I naturally expected to get it, I was that egotistic and confident, after all it was only a job interview; anyone can get any job they want, if they use the right bullshit, simple as that. Anyway, I had weighed the geezer up within two minutes of meeting him, said all the right things he wanted to hear and after five, I knew I had the job.

As I traveled back to our asbestos shed, I could see Carol looking out for me, and when I came into her view, she ran towards me, her pretty face was a picture when I told her I had got the job. She seemed so happy, if not relieved; I suppose she had suffered more than I realised during the last five years in London. It was okay for me to go out and do drugs, steal and be out all hours, but it never entered my head that Carol would not even know if I was coming home or been nicked, stabbed or even killed, plus she had three kids to bring up, so seeing that smile brought it all home to me, it made me appreciate all she had done by getting us all away from London alive and intact. I owe my life to Carol, because if it was not for her then I would have without doubt ended up dead – she saved my life by giving me a simple choice – drugs, crime or your family.

That's how Carol changed my way of thinking, she gave me a choice and it had a tremendous effect on me, and a moment of clarity came to me, it was that strong, it made me put myself in a dingy cold damp bed-sit in mid winter, with not as much as a detox kit for medication or a sleeping tablet, I went cold turkey and climbed the walls for ten days. I chose to do it that way, so that I could really feel the pain of withdrawal and hopefully never forget it and believe me I will never forget that time – it scared the life out of me so much that it had the desired effect on me and that was, that I would never want to use again. So far to date it has worked; I am now free of narcotics and have been for over twenty-seven years.

After the first week, I was due to be paid. I knew it wouldn't be much especially after the tax man had his cut and the fact that I was working under an alias meant I would be taxed to the full limit because I was having to work under an emergency tax code, in other words the robbing bastards took a third of my well-earned honest money. But the only thing on my mind was a piece of rump steak, a bag of coal and a few beers, we had not had meat for a month and I had burnt everything made of wood including the six foot hedge that surrounded the property (asbestos shed) because there was no central heating, only a small hole in the wall which was supposed to be a log burner. I spent most nights in front of that so called log burner, feeding it with anything that would burn just to stop us all dying from bloody hyperthermia.

Carol had all my wages spent before I even got paid; she spent hours writing her shopping list and then kept cutting it back until it became more realistic and affordable. It was the excitement of us having some money after so long on hand-outs, that she started to enjoy working out the housekeeping, she would involve the kids as well and of course, all kids want sweets, so it became a game to them and if they helped her around the shed then they would get a treat. I often think back at how happy the family was at that time even though we never had two bob to rub together. It goes without saying, if you go without for a while, you appreciate more of the small mercies in life, like a bag of coal and a rump steak of course.

'You made a mistake love,' I said to the pay clerk as I tried handing back my wage packet.

'What seems to be the problem John?' she said as she walked over to the counter.

'Check the amount,' I said in a pissed-off, no-nonsense tone.

She looked at the pay slip and read the amount out loud to me and said, 'What seems to be the trouble, John? Fifty hours work, £125, seems all correct to me.'

It dawned on me that she was serious regarding the amount. I had a bit of a shock coming to me when I asked her to explain my wages to me and she told me that I was not earning £125 per day as I first thought, but £125 per week and the fucking taxman was taking a third of that. I was gutted. I worked my bollocks off all that week and all for a miserable pittance. I was now having second thoughts about this so called straight life, how the fuck was I going to stick with this type of life change? I just didn't realise what honest work was about, it had been years since I worked legit and I earned a lot more then, compared to what I was earning here.

The boss came out of his office and approached me after hearing me whining and moaning and said, 'I'm afraid it's Island wages, John,' then he went on to tell me how the Islanders were unofficially paid less than people who live and work on the mainland. My thoughts were that some clever prick, probably a dodgy businessman, created this fucking rule after realising that there was a shortage of jobs on the Island and it has stayed the same ever since.

'Who the fuck invented that load of bollocks?' I said loudly. The boss just looked at me, shocked, because I was now beginning to get loud and all he had seen of me up to this point was this polite, quite easy-going bloke, but now he was seeing a very different character, not a happy bunny I can assure you, especially when that character had thought he had been short changed and was extremely pissed off. For a brief moment whilst I was loudly debating, I had this overwhelming urge to grab the fucker by the throat and march the slippery bastard up to the jug (Bank) to get me what I thought I was owed – thankfully the urge subsided.

It was the second time I felt humiliated and powerless, the first being the incident with H and Billy. I knew if I carried on arguing and playing up that I would lose my job and that would fuck all our plans up, so I had no choice but to swallow hard, but believe me that boss did not realise how close he came to a fucking good hiding.

I explained to Carol what had happened and bless her she cut that shopping list right down and still managed to get my rump steak and bag of coal.

After a fortnight, I was offered the job as paint shop foreman, because I had sussed out how to use the paint properly now so they were hiring more sprayers who were to be trained by me and that meant more money which was desperately needed, so I took the position. After a few months there I became a trusted and respected employee and without being too flash, the work that came out of our workshop was really pucker so the management left me to it get on with the job with no hassle. To be honest, I think the boss remembered what I was like over my wages and probably thought I was best left alone. Anyway, I would often work weekends, which meant I was often on my own at the yard. One Saturday morning I was approached by Simon the bosses' younger brother and junior partner regarding a bit of business. I had sussed this geezer out as a bit dodgy, because in the short time I had been working there I had seen him 'doing business' in the company of what I would call from experience, a few unsavoury people who he had frequently met at odd times in secluded parts of the yard, so I knew he was up to something. I can spot another villain a mile off because we all have a similar characteristic, whether it's the walk, the talk, body language and mannerisms or even the clothes style, there's always something that another villain can notice or identify one of his own, even the police would train their plain clothes officers to act our way. There were some that were very good and were used on some very successful under cover stings, but bear in mind there were some fucking useless ones that stood out like a sore thumb. Simon had obviously spotted me as one of the villainous type and carefully approached me with a little plan to help bump my wages up. Our new car-spraying business had just been founded unbeknown to his brother Miles and it became very popular on the Island, especially because the paint we were using had a guaranteed thirty-year shine, five-year anti-foul protection and only needed one coat and cost two hundred and fifty pounds a litre which proved to be the most advanced and expensive paint on the market. Our dodgy advertisement in the local paper had worked wonders and within a month we had two major car dealers from the mainland, who wanted their part-exchange motors blown over, then they were sent to auction and sold for a much better price – all because of the paint job, it made them look almost brand new. Trouble was, the paint was expensive and Simon couldn't lose anymore from the store, otherwise the firm would have sussed that their stock was dwindling pretty fast and they would soon realise something was wrong and knowing Miles the boss he would probably end up calling old bill and as usual the old bill would have had a whale of a time with me.

The last thing I wanted was to be investigated or arrested by the old bill, because I was working under an alias. It would only take five minutes after they had my prints to find out who I really was and the bastards would have thought they had won the lottery and tried to have me for every crime that they could not solve. In the early eighties I was nicked on the Island, they had me on counterfeiting bank notes for which I got two years. While in their custody they unofficially warned me that if I ever returned or attempted to live on the Island then my life would be made hell – trouble was, my family were now living here and I had to be with them, so for me, family comes first, old bill and their threats come a big second, so it meant sweet fuck all to me. After all, my personal experience with them over the years gave me the opinion that some were more evil and corrupt than the villains on the street. I have had firsthand experience of being arrested, beaten and stitched up in court for no reason and it was for those antics that I hated them. That's why I had to keep a low profile and live and work under an assumed name. Then just as I thought the car spraying business was all over because we could not afford the price of this paint, a bit of unexpected luck was about to come my way.

Duran Duran, the pop band, was quite popular at that time and their lead singer, Simon Le Bon, had become part of the yacht racing clan. He purchased a top of the range ocean going fast yacht. Which was named *Drum* and went on a few racing events; personally, I didn't follow that sport or really did I like it.

We were now down to our last ten litres of paint and had a few dozen eager customers waiting. I was now beginning to panic a bit, when I happened to turn the TV on one evening and the head lines were mentioning Simon Le Bon's yacht, which had capsized in a race and was now being towed into an Isle of Wight boatyard for repairs, my first thoughts were, 'Wanker! Stick to the music.' But the next day whilst at work I saw the tug boat towing *Drum* into the dry dock nearby; it did look a mess, but good old Simon wanted it repaired and re-painted. At that time other companies were becoming aware of this new paint and the type of finish it could produce so good old Simon had decided he wanted the whole yacht painted with it.

About a week later, I'm having a few beers at lunch time in the local pub near to the boat yard, when two geezers approached me and introduced themselves as 'reps for a company that was being considered for the Drum contract, they wanted the same paint used as on our project and of course quite a few cars. They asked if they could join me and have a quick chat regarding a pressing issue. My first thoughts were that these two were old bill and had sussed the car scam, so I just told them to get on with whatever it was that they thought I could do for them. They then asked me if I was familiar with Le Bon and his yacht Drum. I said, 'Vaguely. Why?' and they went on to explain that apparently I was the only qualified person in the area who could use the paint and would I be willing to be part of the contract to paint Le Bon's yacht. I explained that I was already employed but they said that some of the work would be going to my company in return for my services.

The first thing I spoke about was money as there was no fucking way I was painting this pop star's boat for a pittance per week. They asked me how much I wanted; I paused for a moment and told them that I would give them an answer the next day. They tried to get me to make up my mind there and then, but I was having none of it. I think they assumed that I would have jumped at their job offer straight away, but I knew they needed me more than I needed them and I took full advantage of that knowledge and decided to sleep on it.

Once back at the yard, Miles the boss called me in the office who knew of my conversation with the two reps. He said that work at the yard was starting to dry up now because the boat we were building was almost complete and it was now imperative they sell it or they would not have enough capital to build another, so any extra work that came in would help keep the firm afloat. He asked me to work 30 hours per week over at their yard and 20 hours with him for my usual weekly wages.

I said to him straight off, 'I want to work my own deal with them.'

Wearily he replied 'No problem John, just remember what I have just told you and please don't over-price it ok?'

'Okay Miles.' I answered confidently.

I met up with the reps again and asked what they wanted me to do job wise. They explained that the contract required the whole of the yacht to be painted, including the inside. We worked out a deal which was cash in hand for me and I also managed to wangle that Simon took total control, regarding the ordering of the paint and other materials which would be needed, in more ways than they knew.

The paint had to be ordered and flown in from the States, which meant there was to be a reprieve for our car spraying business. The thing about this paint was that if mixed slightly wrong or sprayed at the wrong temperature, the result was crap. The way it worked with the cars was that one coat of this unique paint sprayed over the existing paint without any preparation apart from getting rid of the odd bit of rust and once done, the finish was stunning. That's how we could produce the car work so quickly and cheaply, but you really had to have the knack with what you were doing and for some reason I became very good at using it. I couldn't brag how good I was or otherwise they would have questioned the amount of wastage, which some weeks could be up to twenty litres – at £250 a litre that's a huge loss for them, but they got everything done to schedule and the work was pucker, they expected and allowed for losses and damage, especially on this project as it was the first of its kind.

I was spraying one of the cars in the yard on the Sunday morning, when I saw the boss's younger brother Simon with another yachtie drive a Range Rover into the yard. Straight away I thought they were up to a bit of dodgy business and decided to get a bit nosey. I told the young lad that was working with me to turn everything off and keep quiet until I knew what was going down. Once we had shut everything down, I watched them from the dingy window of our workshop. Out of instinct I watched Simon's body language and it was telling me that this hooray Henry was up to something. I've been about long enough to know what's what and always relied on my gut feeling, except when very desperate. This pair was in a real hurry. They were unloading and carrying boxes from the car quickly up the pontoon on to the Yacht, the whole process took them about ten minutes. As they left, Simon was driving the Range Rover like a get-away driver, they clipped and left a boat which on stands and nearly tipped it over which left it unstable. They just wanted out of that yard as quickly as possible.

My brain was now where it used to be when I was 'At-it' in Peckham and my gut feeling was telling me – 'Go have a look, John'. I got shot of the geezer who was helping me and then when I was alone, I made my way on to the pontoon and boarded the yacht. Once on board, it was like walking into a royal chamber – it even had a Jacuzzi with twenty-two caret gold taps, pure luxury. I had a quick look around, but found no sign of the boxes. So I carried on searching, only this time a bit more thoroughly; I went looking in the 'unusual places'. After having a good look in the master bedroom, I came across them all stacked neatly in a hidden compartment under the wardrobe. I took one of the boxes from the stash over to the bed and opened it up – inside there were rows of small boxes with names that were written in what looked like pharmaceutical jargon to me. I opened up a few more boxes and found different types of drugs, boxed like they were ready for the shop counter. My knowledge of illegal drugs is exceptional, considering I had firsthand experience of using and selling them in the past, but this stuff had me baffled. I closed the opened boxes so they looked untouched and returned them to the compartment after I had written down the names that were printed on the packaging.

I went straight from the yard to a geezer I had got friendly with in our local, an old bloke who was a retired schoolteacher; he was typical of his ex-profession when he spoke to you and some of the locals did not like him for that, that's why we probably got on because we had something in common. He was also very knowledgeable in various fields, so I rolled off a few names that had been on the boxes, telling him a bull shit story.

He said straight away, 'Young man, please stay clear of that poison.'

I asked him, 'Why?'

'Steroids young man, are one of life's accelerators Stay well clear dear boy and use the gym as it should be used.' Then he went on to tell me a story about some young geezer and what this shit had done to him, who for me was knowledgeable and interesting, but I never had any intentions of taking them, only selling them.

My brain was racing now and I made a call to a good pal in London who was in the know and had good contacts. Later that day he found out what this gear came to price wise and what I was told was an eye opener. This stuff, if it's quality, can cost more than Charlie, so I knew that I was on to an earner here when he actually offered to take as much as I could get hold of. But first I would have to plan something very quick; because I had no idea how long the stuff would be aboard the Yacht.

I went straight back to the boat yard and went on board, and then I made a list of everything that was there, phoned London and got a sale price. I was looking at £20,000 wholesale price or £30,000 on the street. I was really sweating on this one because I needed this pay day badly especially after the ball's up I made with H' and Billy. The thing I had to be careful about on this one was that Simon knew me, he knew where I lived and knew I was dodgy, what he didn't know, was that I was working there under an alias name and if for some reason they happened to be legit then old bill could be called in and if so I could be in big trouble. But the most important thing for me was that I had promised Carol I would stay straight – my gut feeling, though, was telling me that Simon & Co were at it, and having them over would be okay because I could easily justify it, in my eyes they were 'at it' and sometimes people who are 'at it' come unstuck. It's a dog-eat-dog business and apart from that, if I'm to be honest, I was pissed off being skint and fucking bored with the scam I was working with the cars. I had no idea who Simon & Co were doing business with, so I had to be extra careful. I must have smoked twenty fags and drank half a bottle of brandy before I came up with a scam, I decided to ring Simon and get him to meet me at the yard. I told him a bollocks story on the phone and it was enough to get him down there.

I was waiting at the main gates when he arrived and asked him to follow me into the paint store. I was concocting a story about the paint he had ordered and that it was now useless because someone had fucked with the temperature gauge in the paint store. He knew how volatile the paint could be and if it gets fucked, then you're talking thousands of pounds and this geezer was money orientated. I just wanted him in that store room with just me, with no witnesses. The building was quite soundproof and it only had one way in and out which suited my plan to a tee I had always in the past been able to put the fear of God into people whilst I was on a bit of work – it was better than beating the shit out of them.

I could change my mood, looks, and especially my eyes, when I gave what I call 'the look'. There were people that just broke down and gave me whatever it was that I was after. To me it was much better than hurting some unfortunate geezer, so I classed myself as a civilised villain. But with the profession I was in I had to be fucking willing to hurt people if they didn't cooperate – believe me, if I was on a piece of work and I was looking at 20 years if I got caught, then I would go to any lengths to get my prize. I was mentioned and described once as a complete gentleman robber when a victim made their statement to the old bill. I had a good laugh over that. It pays to try and pacify your target and assure them that if they follow your demands, then life will be a bowl of cherries for them.

I was ready for Simon and wanted him under my control quickly, so he would have no time to think. I wanted him confused and mixed up. As he entered the store I was right behind him and once the door was shut, I cracked him a beauty of a punch to his kidney area –

instantly he went down and tried his hardest to yell and scream, but when you're caught with one of those punches you can't even breathe let alone cry out, the pain can be awesome, a fit boxer can be floored with that punch. Our Ricky Hatton uses that punch and he is in my opinion the best at administering it, he knows the exact spot.

Before he could move I grabbed him by his jacket lapels and brought my face within two inches of his. The look I gave him brought complete terror to his face. I growled at him, 'Don't say a fucking word and listen very carefully to what I have to say Simon.' This silly fucker takes no notice of what I have just said to him and tries his hardest to shout out and get up onto his feet, only this time I brought my clenched fist down very hard on the top of his head, similar to a hammer blow – the effect is more like a thump rather than a punch because you're not using the knuckle part of the hand. If done correctly it gives you concussion but leaves no lumps and you're totally fucked, a tactic I picked up from the metropolitan police, they were experts at using it. I pulled the prick into a sitting position and noticed his eyes were rolling. I knew from my boxing days that concussion had set in and it would be several minutes before I would get any sense out of him. To kill time, I decided to tie his hands behind his back and pulled a small stool up so that I would be sitting facing him when he came to.

It took a minute or so for him to focus and realise his situation. When he came round enough to talk he said in a self pitying chitty-chat patter, 'What is going on? Why have you attacked me John? Why am I tied?'

I just sat on that stool and stared at him, not saying a fucking word, it was all part of the play-act to me, I've used this tactic a number of times. I needed him to think that I knew more than he thought, so I played the part in quiet mode. My silence had the right effect, it done his fucking head in and after a few minutes he began to get louder. I slapped him hard with the palm of my hand each time his voice got louder. This geezer had no idea why this was happening to him and he was terrified; as far as he knew, I could have been a complete psycho who wanted to kill him. He only knew me as one of his employees and of course the car scam but he had no real idea who I really was, only now he was about to find out who he was dealing with. I now knew that I had total control over him as he was now doing his best in trying to patronise me, saying all types of bollocks and promises. As he drabbled on and on, I casually rolled an extra large fag, lit it, then I leant over as if to whisper in his ear and then stuck the red hot end in his ear. The fucker nearly hit the roof and his screams were really high pitched, a bit like a horror movie actress just encountering Count Dracula.

I instantly slapped him and put my hand over his mouth. I pushed my face right up to his and said very calmly, 'Do you now understand what I am saying to you?' He managed to nod a 'Yes' then I went on to tell him to shut up and listen. 'You have a simple choice here Simon – do as you're told and all will be okay or, if you think you're clever and tell me a load of bollocks, I will break your legs.' I then took my hand away from his mouth and he became quiet as a mouse. I said, 'I've known of the scam for some time and I've seen what's been going on, but most important, what you don't know is that your little firm and your scam have upset certain well respected infamous people, who want you and your firm out of business and out of the way. It's as simple as that, matey,' which I said in an Island accent with a smirk look on my face just to be sarcastic. I then smacked him hard across the face and grabbed him by the throat and said impatiently, 'Listen, you prick, I'm here to fuck you up; I've been sent here especially to do you harm and put you out of business, so do you understand what I have just said?' He nodded. I said to him, 'You have £30,000 street value stored in that boat and the people you have stepped on, want something done to you – now I would consider what reply you give me to the next few questions, because if I think that you're not giving me an honest answer, then I will hurt you very badly as promised, so you have a choice dear boy.'

He panicky said, 'Take it all, it is all yours, just don't hurt me. I will do anything you say, just don't hurt me.'

I knew I had this prick exactly where I wanted him, powerless! He would have kissed my arse if I asked him. I started again with the play-act and said, 'How much are you willing to pay, for me not to hurt you? Remember I am being paid a good price for this. And I wondered what price you think its worth for me not to hurt you?'

He said, 'I can give you the buy money, which is fifteen grand, but I am being honest when I say that I would need time to get the cash and as for the shipment, even though I said take it, in fact, it would be wise to leave it untouched because I can afford to lose the fifteen grand but not the shipment. If that goes, then all sorts of trouble will happen for me and I would probably end up missing. I am a married man with two kids, so I am pleading with you John, for their sake.'

I just stared a menacing look at him without losing eye contact and he never looked away, I knew I just had a result and therefore I should just give him the illusion that he was winning me over. I knew he was being honest, but I could not probe too much, or he may suss that something was not right; after all, I was just bluffing my way through this and was doing quite well. 'Never get greedy, Macky boy, or you'll come unstuck, son,' were sound words given to me by one of the Great train robbers whilst I was doing a bit of bird in Brixton prison and I never forgot advice like that. I rolled another fag while sitting only a few feet away and instantly I could see the panic in his eyes. He was probably thinking I would repeat what I had done to him earlier. I just took a long drag on the fag and half smiled at him as I blew the smoke into his face, paused for a minute, then said, 'Okay, I'll leave your shipment with you, but I want the buy money today.'

He started whining on about how awkward it could be if he took that amount of money from where he had it stashed. I reacted instantly and I just smacked him a real hard one across his face which stopped his jabbering in its tracks. He had to realise that I was the one who was in charge and not to give me stupid excuses.

I said to him angrily, 'Well Simon improvise, you prick, think and use that so called privately paid for educated grey matter of yours.

You have five minutes to come up with something that will make me a happy bunny, I think you know what will make me happy, so think about it very carefully, okay?'

He gave me a meek look and nod. It didn't take him long to come back to me with an idea; it's amazing how the brain works when it's under pressure. When I got a pull from old bill, which use to be often in London, I learnt very quickly how to react – when I was on the ball I could surprise myself with what came out of my mouth, especially if they believed me.

He said he would have to use the phone to speak to his sister. I said, 'Can she get the cash?'

He said, 'She is the only one that could help, but I cannot guarantee it, because it is so short notice.'

I said 'Your sister? Is she involved with your scam?'

He said, 'No John, I give you my word, she only keeps cash for us and sends it offshore to the Cayman Islands. She has no idea that it is buy money or what we are doing. She just thinks we are fiddling the tax man and putting it in a safe place. Remember, this yacht we are constructing is the first of its kind. That means it is a prototype and we have had lots of investment to get this project off the ground, so if we don't succeed in selling it, then the firm goes bust and the way things are going, which is what will be happening. The Southampton boat show is our last hope and if that fails we go bust and everyone loses their investments, or as an alternative we will take her out in the middle of the med and sink her, that way the investors get something back via insurance.'.

I realised that this geezer and his brother were quite smart, what we call in the game, 'white collar thieves' and they had probably set this whole thing up as an insurance scam if the boat didn't take off. This boat, if it sold, would fetch over two million pounds and if they got a contract to build a few then they were looking at raking in millions. But these geezers were into other things to cover their own arses, only now, unlucky for them, they had me to contend with.

I had realised that I was enjoying this piece of work, I had been at it' for most of my life up until a few months ago. Since then I had been in the process of trying to change my wicked ways. Well, I thought to myself, here I am doing what I do best yet again. I have always attracted trouble or found myself in deep shit many times. I would always promise Carol that I would steer clear of any trouble, even though I really meant it, I could guarantee something would always happen. I was a magnet to agro. I realised many years later why it was always me it happened to, but more of that later.

I said to him, 'Have you got the keys to the office?'

He replied that there was a spare set hidden outside the office.

'Right, on your feet and get the spare keys.' I pulled him up because his hands were still tied. I pushed him to the door of the paint store and opened the door to just take a look to make sure no one was about, even though it was closed over the weekend, you just never knew and seeing I was a magnet to trouble I was being careful. I said to him, 'Sweet, let's go! And no fucking nonsense or you will go fucking missing, did you get that?'

'John I will be fine, just please don't hurt me anymore.'

'Well, I'll leave that one up to you,' I growled.

It was only a few metres to the office. He pointed out to me where the keys were. Once in the office, I sat him in this big leather swivel chair and picked the phone up and put it to his ear. I said to him after he gave me the number 'Be fucking careful what you say and how you say it or I swear I'll rip you a new arsehole,' and dialed the number.

The phone rang for a while before he got an answer, 'Judith, thank God I caught you in.' He then explained to her that fifteen grand was needed that day and could she not mention anything to Miles, his brother. She spoke for about two minutes and I couldn't quite make out what she was saying. 'No, I am not back gambling again, this is strictly a business deal and the money will be replaced by next week.' But he was adamant with her that his brother was not being told anything.

She agreed to meet him with the money in an hour at the boatyard. I told him that when she arrived, to keep it short and not too get angry with her if she starts asking too many questions, because it was a dead cert she would say something. I untied him when I heard her car. She drove into the yard and parked up and I noticed she was carrying an A4 size envelope under her arm. She was a looker, well dressed but you could tell she was of a different breed, probably never had a good fuck in her life and never been in love, the type that marries a nerd for money, has a couple of kids, lots of affairs then Bamm! It's divorce time! She gets the house, half the dough and the kids get packed off to boarding school then she tries to find the perfect life with the perfect partner, all bollocks in my opinion. I went into the adjoining office with the door on the jar. She came in and started asking him questions; he handled her quite well and gave her a good enough storyline for her to be satisfied and she left okay.

As soon as I heard her car door shut, I came back into the office. The envelope was still where his sister had left it, Simon had swivelled his chair in the direction of the window, which overlooked the River Medina. He was just sitting quietly and staring at nothing, almost meditational. I picked up the envelope and ripped it open and there were three bundles of twenty pound notes, all with a seal and the amount around them.

It felt real good to have some real cash again; especially after I had been earning crap money and if it had not been for the fiddle with the cars then fuck knows how we would of have survived. I congratulated Simon on the way he handled his Sister, 'Well done, you done well and I'll keep to my word, okay?'

He said, 'You promise?'

I gave him the look and roared at him and told him that if I gave my word, then my word is my bond. 'Ask me again and I might think you don't believe me, and then if that happens I might just change my mind.'

He said, 'Look, I'm very sorry for doubting your word. I have never been in this situation before. I only got involved because Miles was worried we would lose all we have if the boat did not attract buyers. He made it all sound so simple when we first started, now look at the mess I am in.'

'Listen,' I said. 'I'll keep my people sweet and you get rid of your stock as usual, then return the fifteen grand to your sister and I will make arrangements for someone to stop you getting your supplies and considering you must pay up front, there's a thousand ways to cover your problem. Your brother will be thinking a completely different reason as to why he can't buy his next shipment and the loss of your next buy money – and one last bit of advice. Stay clear of this sort of business in the future because, you're way out of your league. Go and get a proper job.' I then reminded him that if the firm was to go bust, then I was to be the last to go job wise.

He looked at me strangely and said, 'I suppose you want to make sure there's no more business being done, John.'

I said to him, 'Something like that Simon, but you make sure I'm the last to go, okay?'

He just nodded a yes and I recommended he got some TCP antiseptic liquid for his ear. I was just being a smarmy bastard really and left him sitting in his chair.

I left the yard and made my way to my local; it was more like an old people's home and the conversations I had with the locals were complete bollocks to me; it was either boats or vegetables. What the fuck did a geezer from Peckham know about that shit? I felt I had landed on the fucking moon some days. It wasn't until I had that earner in my pocket that I realised I had not had a puff (cannabis) in a long while and I could have done with a joint to bring me down from the high I had been feeling, but here on the Island I knew no one who I could score from, so I started drinking every day. I needed a buzz, I could not live this groundhog life anymore without that warm calming feeling I craved when I was on the gear. Within a month I was on the Special Brew, sickening syrup supposed to be lager which was quite strong and the first one would always taste awful but by the time you were on the second pint it tasted like the best cocktail ever made. It got my head to where it wanted to be and in some ways it enabled me to be tolerant and quite happy to talk bollocks with the locals, even if the feeling was only temporary.

I found it difficult mixing and being around these people. To be honest I found them fucking resentful and biased to people like me because we came from the mainland. Most were blatantly rude and ignorant. It didn't take me long to realise that these caulk heads were tight as a duck's arse and most would fucking stab you in the back as soon as your back was turned, but more about that later.

I stayed in the pub till closing time which was ten thirty – that was a piss take, fucking half past ten. I'd be just going out, not coming home if I was back in Peckham. But here I was trying to be a changed man and fuck me, I had no idea what was in store for my family and me over the next coming years. I left the boozer after buying every tight fucker a drink and started making my way back to the family shed, which was what I jokily called our home and then suddenly I realised I hadn't got any coal from the shop, which had been closed since five pm. There was no way I could stand another night in that shit hole freezing my arse off. I was worried about my Danny, he was only a baby and both Carol and I would make sure he was warm by leaving the gas cooker on.

Only now, I was half pissed, had no coal and a load of money on me. I would have to explain to Carol where it had come from. Carol and the kids must have been freezing and wondering where I had got to. I really felt bad about that because I was being uncaring and selfish, just because I wanted a buzz to feel different and let some steam off. I got that buzz sat with a load of back stabbers talking gibberish. My mind was already dreaming up some fantastic alibi, something amazing that could only happen to me and hope Carol would swallow it and not give me a hard time. As I wobbled home I decided to take a piss in someone's driveway. As I'm doing the business, I noticed a wheelbarrow full of cut logs just inside the drive; I just looked up to the sky and just said, 'Thanks, God, that's handy.'

I knew instantly that this barrow of logs were not heaven sent because as soon as I moved it, the wheel made the sound of a strangled rat. Squeak! Squeak! And I had only got about three metres and that night you could hear a pin drop, so as I went faster, with the barrow it went squeak, squeak and fucking louder squeaks the faster I went. Logs began to fall off as I went over an open grass area. I was so determined we all would not freeze that night, I even stopped to pick them up, it was dawning on me what I was doing and said out loud, 'What the fuck am I doing?'

I thought, what would happen if I got nicked for this? Over on the Island, if you pissed in a doorway, you would end up in the local paper and that thought made me run like fuck. As I got to the rear of the shed home, I saw Carol looking over what was left of our hedge at me in a funny way, I thought that's a result; at least she wasn't growling.

She said comically 'What the bloody hell have you gone and done now? Where did those logs come from? In fact, where the hell have you been?'

I just said, 'It's a long story love. I forgot the coal and happened to bump into this barrow full of logs on the way home, 'honest babe'

She just smiled and walked back into the shed. She knew me too well and seeing this one time respected villain coming home with a wheelbarrow full of logs amused her more, rather than getting angry with me. We never froze that night and Carol never asked me anymore about the day and she went off to bed. I sat in front of the fire with a drink and went over what I had actually done that day. I didn't want to tell Carol a bullshit story seeing that I was half pissed that night, it would only make her feel that there was more to what I was telling her, so I decided to sleep on it and think things through the next day. I didn't surface until gone eleven, which was unusual for me, my head was pounding and I felt like shit, all down to the booze. As soon as I pulled back the blankets, all five of them, I felt the cold instantly; I would always shower and get dressed when I was back in Peckham, mind you we had central heating there, but here, it felt as if we had gone back to Victorian times and had to dress before we could wash because it was so fucking cold.

Carol managed to get this temporary shed to live in through the council housing department only until a flat or house became available. Prior to that, she and our three kids were put in a one room bed & breakfast-come-hotel accommodation for quite some time until she complained; they then offered her and the kids the asbestos shed in East Cowes. This all happened while I was getting clean from the smack and the crack back in London. The shed they offered her had been derelict for some time and was partially under water due to some scum bag nicking the lead pipe.

The shed, was to Carol a palace; I could not accept that I would have to start all over again in a fucking freezing shed. My efforts to try to change were something that I could not talk about, even to Carol, especially when I felt lost and confused and it was years later that I learnt the reason why I felt change was so hard, it was that simple if I was to become honest with myself and that was a hard job on its own for me. I later found out it was all down to my ego and pride. I learnt the hard way of course, but more of that later.

I told Carol a bollocks story, that the bosses were so impressed with my work that they took me out and got me pissed, I went on and said that they were going to give me a bonus. Carol's eyes lit up when the word bonus was mentioned because I already had been telling her that the company might be closing down and I could be out of work. I put a grand on the table and told her that when I was out with them and once they were half pissed, I just happened to mentioned that I needed a car and got them to give me some cash up front so I could get a motor. It was all complete bollocks! I desperately wanted to say, 'Look babe, I've just had one of the bosses over for fifteen grand but don't worry about it.' She would automatically think I had robbed the local post office or bank.

So I lied, I lied to keep the peace, but today I now know that was just a justification. I went up to London a few weeks later to buy a car at the auctions and came back with a Volvo and most important of all, it had a blinding heater. I laugh to myself now, because we would all sit in the car with the engine running with the heater on full blast because it was the warmest we had all felt since leaving Peckham.

Monday morning came and I had to go into work as usual. We would normally get in ten minutes before we were due to start work so we could have a coffee and a chat; the usual topic would be who won at darts or who was growing the biggest vegetable. I had started to accept that my days as a Peckham villain were over along with the buzz and excitement I had grown accustomed to since I was ten years of age. These people knew nothing about me or my past and on some occasions whilst drinking with them after work, I would, after a few pints, start telling a few stories, mainly about people I knew and what they had done. Their faces were a picture when I was in full flow; they had never heard of anything like I had been telling them. Most of the wankers never believed half of what I had said because we had lived totally different lives. My life in London could not be explained to them, they had no concept of my upbringing and background, and it would be all pie in the sky to them. They would never be able to believe nor accept it. It would be Hollywood movie stuff to them. I felt completely alien with these people; we were so different in every shape or form.

Miles, the boss, rolled in at his usual time at about nine and there was no sign of his brother Simon. I was thinking, maybe he has told his brother, or maybe they were up to something. I suppose I was a bit paranoid. I carried on working as usual, when Miles came into our spray shop.

'Morning, John,' he said as he walked passed me to pick up a table top that had been painted a few days before.

I said to him, 'Morning, Miles. Want a hand with that?'

His reply told me he knew fuck all about what had happened. 'If you don't mind, John, because it is a bit of a heavy lump.'

As I helped him pick the table top up, I asked, 'Where's Simon today, Miles?'

He laughed as he said, 'He got pissed over the weekend and fell on the log burner.'

I asked to give the impression that I was really concerned for his welfare. 'Is he okay? Has he been hurt?'

Miles laughed again and said, 'The silly bugger had burnt his ear on the burner and now it has got infected, so he is at the hospital.'

I laughed as I said, 'He needs to give the rum up mate, or it could have been his arse or even his dick.'

Miles just laughed as we carried the table top.

I felt good now because good old Simon had kept schtum, so the play act had worked. As I said before, it's much better than beating the shit out of someone, unless you're a complete psycho like Billy, who got pleasure from hurting people. I know I dished a bit out on the geezer, but it was either that or half kill the fucker, he had to be scared shitless and that was exactly how I got him without being too nasty. To be honest I think he had a result – if he had been stroppy with me, he wouldn't have been complaining about a burnt ear, it would have been more like, 'Where's my fucking ear?' Anyway pricks like him and his brother should have stuck to boats and the stock market and stay clear of drug dealing – they wouldn't have lasted five minutes back in Peckham.

Within a few weeks of the Southampton boat show, I noticed the investors were at the boat yard having long meetings with the two brothers and a few came from the Channel Islands, so I thought its crunch time for this firm. The other lads at the yard had gathered that something was up and the Chinese whispers started spreading with like wild fire, like if they were to keep their jobs or who would get laid off first. It was strange watching these Islanders react to this situation; firstly I noticed that every conversation regarding the future of their jobs got totally exaggerated, then I saw most of them kiss arse and people please the two bosses. It wasn't long before the back stabbing started and the way they went about it was fucking pathetic, it was like watching kids play up at school. A meeting was arranged, to explain to us all what was happening. They basically said to us all

'Find yourselves another job.' Within a week half the work force was laid off and that included my staff in the spray shop. The 'Drum project went out of the window as well, but I wasn't that bothered about it really as I was now pissed off with spraying boats. Simon avoided me as much as possible, probably because he was shit scared of me and felt humiliated even when we did bump into each other he would be nice as pie and neither one of us never ever mentioned what had happened, which suited me fine.

Around a month later, I was the only one left at the firm and I would basically take the piss when only Simon was in the office. I'd take three hour lunch breaks in the local or if I knew Miles was away, then I would stay home and still expect to get paid. I now knew it was time to move on and do something with the dough I had stashed. I walked into Simon's office and said to him bluntly, 'Simon the Drum contract seems to be going nowhere so 'I'm off, but please remember our little chat okay?' He just looked at me and I sensed he was totally relieved and a smile came to his face, he even shook my hand as he eagerly agreed. Carol was impressed with the fact that I was the last geezer to get laid off; she expected Island attitudes to kick in and that I would be the first to go, but being the last to go tallied with the story I had told her earlier to account for the extra money that I acquired and the fact that the bosses liked me and my work was superb and had held onto me for as long as they could.

I could never tell her I had fifteen grand – she would never have swallowed that – so I told her it was three grand which sounded more realistic or should I say believable. For the next few weeks we just enjoyed being together and seeing that the weather was improving, we would drive all over the Island and stop for pub lunches. Carol never asked for much and a drive around the Island was really enjoyable for her and if she was happy then I was too. We had a bit of luck when a letter from the council housing arrived, saying that we had been allocated a three bedroom flat in a place called Preston Close near Ryde. The first thing I said to Carol was, 'It better have flipping central heating.' I didn't give a toss about anything else or even where it was located and getting out of that fucking shed was beyond a relief.

It was becoming usual for me to pop down the pub, only this time I was there to celebrate getting another place. 'Preston Close?' is what the barman replied when I told him that I was moving there, but he said it loudly and the look on his face was giving me the impression that Preston Close was not a popular place.

I asked the barman, 'Well, what's wrong with the place? The look on your face is telling me that I'm being sent to a labour camp or something similar.'

He answered straight back, 'What's right with it! is the question you should be asking. Johnny'

I had a chat with a few of the locals regarding the area of our new address to be. I had learnt that it was where they put all the scum bag problem families; well I had been born and bred on council estates and living amongst scum bags wouldn't be a problem for our family, so I went along with my old man to have a look at the place. When we arrived I was surprised that this estate was only small and it looked nice and had some beautiful views. We were on the top floor of the block; the place had three bedrooms, a big spacious living and dining room, in fact I was over the moon with it.

On the way out to the car one of the locals asked, 'You the new tenants?' It was like looking at someone from the sixties or seventies; he had the mullet hair cut, the clothes, the lot.

I just said to him, 'Do I know you mate? Who are you?'

He was a bit taken back by my reaction to his question and went on to say, 'My name's Darren and I live opposite the block you were in.' He went on to tell me and my old man that the last tenant had hanged himself in our new place.

'Well, Dad, that geezer that hanged himself has done us all a favour, in a roundabout way.' The old man just gave me a weird smirk back. When I told Carol about the place, she was chuffed to see me smiling about it because we had lived in some shit holes in our time and with me smiling, she knew it was okay. We settled in quite easily,

Carol got the kids' schools sorted and I bought a load of furniture and carpets off a geezer who lived on the ground floor, including an electric cooker. Within a week of moving onto the housing estate, I'd found a dodgy butcher worker who would supply me every week with 30kg or more of top quality beef. I already found the local pub and was in there daily, so I had my meat and customers sorted from the regulars.

I decided to swap the existing cooker over to the electric one I had bought earlier. At the time, we had an old pre war gas one. Anyway, I swapped the cookers over and carried the old one down four floors to be collected later. I thought to myself, I'll cook Carol and I a nice steak dinner for when she gets home. I cut two thick juicy steaks off a big joint and put them under the grill. I had never used electric before and thought it will take a bit of time to warm up the grill. By this time I was drinking everyday and I noticed that sometimes I would get annoyed about stupid things which would sometimes make me angry and lose my temper.

But this day was to be an exceptionally negative one for me. I had the day all planned, the dinner, the cooker and even bought some flowers for Carol. Throughout our marriage I always bought her flowers because I was a bit of a romantic at heart and loved her to bits. Getting back to the cooker, I had been in the other room for at least twenty minutes drinking a can and watching the TV and thought I can't smell anything or hear the steak sizzling.

With steak under a grill, you'd expect to get a whiff of the aroma of the meat being grilled slowly, especially after twenty minutes; I thought I would just check the cooker to make sure I had turned it on. I'm in the kitchen the next minute looking at two raw pieces of steak, straight away I checked the plug and that was okay, and then I checked the O rings to see if they were working and, guess what, they were ice cold, now I started to get the hump with this so-called modern top of the range cooker. I spent an hour taking the 30 amp plug out of the wall checking all the wiring, yet I couldn't find a fucking thing wrong with the work I had done. I then came to the conclusion that it was the cooker that was fucked and within seconds my mind was already made up and I'm out the front door and I flew down the stairs knocking on the geezer's door who had sold it to me.

After ten minutes of banging on his door, I suddenly thought, 'Fucking hell, it's getting late and Carol and the kids would be back soon and the new cooker is fucked. Lucky for me our old gas cooker one was still where I had left it and to be perfectly honest, I didn't carry it all the way down the stairs. Basically I rolled the pre war piece of crap down the stairs but I did carry it a bit as well. Well, I thought – bollocks, now I'll have to carry the fucker up four floors then fit it back in. Believe me when I say that I was now steaming, I had gone completely red eyed and started kicking the door of the fucker who had sold it to me.

I went out the back of our block of flats and picked up what was left of the old one, well to be honest it looked like that it had been kicked off the top of a sky scraper and looked a mess, then I'm thinking – what if this one don't work either, my mind was all over the place now. So I was now getting louder with the insults at the geezer even though he wasn't in but I knew the neighbours were and as soon as he had got home the nosey fuckers would have warned him, but that was exactly what I wanted. When I eventually got the cooker back inside our flat, I was knackered and the thought of re-fitting this piece of shit just made me go berserk. I had now convinced myself that the geezer had taken me for a mug and if that happens to me, which is rare; my mind would go into blackout mode and I would end up not having a clue what I was doing or what I had done. What I remember vividly was the whole cooker including the built in the wall 30 amp plug and fuse just being ripped out off the wall, bringing half the wall with it as I dragged it towards the front door, then that's when it went blurry.

The rest was told to me later by my neighbours, apparently I threw it down two flights of stairs, calling the cooker by the geezer's name. I then began to jump, kick and beat this thing as if it was the actual geezer – fucking good job he was at work otherwise I think that

I may have just killed him. So my blackout temper was being taken out on this piece of junk. Apparently, they told me I threw it down each flight of stairs shouting all types of obscenities then I would jump from the top flight straight onto it, beating, kicking and then picking the thing up, what was left of it and repeating the same madness on the next landing. I think every tenant on that estate could hear me in full flow. Once I had thrown it down the last flight of stairs, it was half the original size and resembled a crushed car, I left it right outside the geezers' front door. I was told that I waited some time outside his door giving the remains of the cooker a few more kicks and a few more obscenities and then went back upstairs, it was not long before I calmed down and soon realised I had been in blackout, to be honest it frightened the life out of me.

Carol came back with the kids; it was obvious that they had all walked past what was left of our top of the range cooker and Carol had never seen me go berserk, not even in Peckham. 'What's happened babe?' she said in a worried but caring way. I was sitting at our bench in the dining room with a can of special brew in hand; probably my ninth or tenth and with that amount of booze in me I would start to justify what I had done with the bullshit excuses.

I never told Carol about the blackout, but told her that the geezer had fucked us over for the cooker, then totally exaggerated to her how hard it was getting it down the stairs and having to carry our old one back up. I had cuts all over my hands where I smashed the fuck out of the thing. I told Carol I cut them carrying the cookers up and down the stairs, just to get her to believe and feel sorry for me. I suppose I was at that self-pity, poor me stage, I know that today, but then, my thinking was all over the place.

I said to Carol, 'I've had enough of these arseholes, I need another drink to calm me down,' as if nine or ten had not succeeded. I went on to moan at her that I'd rather be away for the evening, just in case I ended up doing the geezer damage. I made my way down the stairs and saw blood which I presumed was my own also there were chunks out of the walls all the way down the stair way, but worse of all was the iron banister rail, I remember thinking to myself 'how the hell did I do that? And not even remember doing it. The bottom rail was bent and twisted and had come loose from its concrete base. Then I saw the cooker, it was in a terrible mess, thank God that geezer was out because in that state of mind I could have killed him. I had already convinced myself that I had not seen him and vaguely remember him being out; also if I had done him, then the old bill would be everywhere.

Once in my local, the owner, a geezer called Jamie asked me straight away, 'What the fuck has happened to your hands mate?' I gave him a bullshit answer, saying I fell through a window. He was an okay geezer who I liked immensely and he got out his first aid kit and sorted me out with plasters and bandages. I ended up falling out of that pub in the early hours. Once home I just climbed into bed and Carol turned her back to me, which was not a good sign but I was so pissed, that I fell unconscious in seconds. The next morning I got up quite late and the house was deserted, my head was thumping like a jack hammer and I was dehydrated. I swallowed four aspirin tablets with a can of special brew and this was ten in the morning, then finished the whole can in one go; I then instantly spewed the lot up even the aspirins. I was really angry with myself, not for drinking that time in morning; but for the fact that I wasted a can that would have given me that warm good feeling buzz I needed to face the day. Now I would have to drink another from my stash.

I was really concerned about my behaviour the day before and decided to go to the doctor's and have a chat about the blackout because I was worried that I lost time and completely had no recognition of what I had done. I went for the appointment and met a quack of a doctor. Two minutes after I poured my heart out to him as honestly as I could, including the excessive amount I was drinking. I have never been as truthful to anyone as I was to him on that day, being that truthful was extremely hard for me to do.

Then this quack tells me, 'Mr. Mack you are extremely depressed and I want you to take this new antidepressant wonder drug and you will feel like a new man in a month.' not once did he mention my drinking.

As I was walking out of the surgery, I remembered reading about this 'new wonder drug' after guinea pig trails were completed in the USA; it was proclaimed the drug of the century. But my opinion of it now is that it is just another chemically induced drug which gives the user a good feel feeling; basically it's a fucking drug. My own diagnosis was, 'I'm depressed because I had recently come off the skag and crack, moved to this boring Island, had no real mates or anyone on my wavelength and I'm living amongst these rednecks on a rock. That was my answer and my reason as to why I drank so much, had blackouts and got angry. I had read years later in the tabloids about this so-called wonder drug being used and prescribed frequently by doctors as if they were Smarties. Then after a time a minority of users would end up wanting to commit suicide or end up completely dependent on them and end up pretty fucked up. In my opinion, they're legit addicts, simple as that and it's fucking legal and these corporate companies that produce and sell it earn fucking millions, so again my opinion of those companies is that they are just white collar drug cartels and should be based in South America along with the coca growers.

I spoke with Carol about what happened at the doctor's, when she interrupted me half way and said, 'John, the geezer who sold us the cooker wasn't ripping us off, he is genuine, you're the one who got it wrong.'

I was getting annoyed with her now because it seemed she was siding with him. 'How would you know, babe? You have never had to deal with these fuckers before, so how can you be so cock sure you're right?'

She came face to face with me and said, 'I've avoided you all day because you're going off your nut John.'

I said in a cocksure way 'Well answer the question love?'

She slowly and methodically told me that the man's whole family were petrified of me and were in hiding.

I told her, 'So they fucking should be, having a skanky bastard like him as an old man.'

Carol said, 'No, John, you're wrong. He came and spoke to me while you were at the pub and he simply explained that the reason nothing worked on the cooker was because you had fucked with all the controls and by doing so you put the timer on delay, that's why it never worked.'

I was lost for words. I just went and sat down all solemn and said, 'Are you sure Carol? He might be working you.'

She said to me in an almost child like way, 'Sweetheart, you're not in Peckham anymore. These people here are completely different from the ones you knew back in Peckham, that's why you are like this, you can't replace the past, so accept this new life or you will go mad. The geezer showed me the timer and it was all down to you having no patience.'

I said, 'I don't believe this, I must be fucking cursed or something. I better go and see him.'

'Bloody right you should,' she said. 'I'm not having the same shit here as we had in Peckham.'

Next day, I made my apologies to the geezer, not that it was sincere, but my thinking was, at least I had made the effort. After, I was just sitting in the front room of our flat in deep thought, when Carol returned from taking the kids to school. She said, 'you okay, babe?'

I said, 'Not really, babe. I've been thinking of what that quack said and these anti-depressants.'

Caringly she calmly said, 'Listen honey-bunch, the doctor knows best. If you've told him the truth about how you're feeling, then he must know what is best for you. Just try and trust and see if it helps okay sweetheart?' I'd have done anything really, so when Carol said it like that, it seemed that she really did care, even though the amount of agro I had caused her so I decided to give it a shot. That afternoon, I'm at the chemist's picking up my so-called wonder drug. I had and still have, deep resentment against mind-altering drugs since going cold turkey from skag and crack. It was a form of hatred I had acquired for all that unnecessary pain I had dished out to others and suffered while on the gear and it was that hatred that was keeping me alive and still is to some extent to this day, but its a hatred I'm reluctant to let go of. Half-heartedly I started taking the medication and after several days I began to feel slightly different. It was more like a laid back type of feeling. One morning I had to go out to deliver some flyers for our newly formed cleaning company Carol and I had decided to start up. We sat down that morning and planned our routes to where we would start delivering. I dropped Carol off in an area close to where we lived and I went a little further afield. I had been driving for a short while, when all of a sudden I had what I can only explain as a terrifying panic attack. I pulled over to the side of the road and my panicky brain thought – what the fuck is it, that I am meant to be doing? Flyers and leaflets were spread all over the passenger seat and I never had a clue at what I was meant to be doing with them nor did I know where I was, when in fact, the area I was in, I knew quite well.

I have to be honest and admit I was shit scared all the time it lasted; it probably lasted about five minutes. My brain was working like a washing machine on 'spin' setting then as quickly as a flash, my memory came flooding back. 'Fuck me! What's happening to me?' I shouted out in the cab of the van. 'What was that all about?' It took a few minutes to get myself together and then carried on with the leaflet delivery. I met up with Carol later on and we went and had a drink at my local. I never mentioned anything to her about the loss of memory, probably because she would think that I was losing the plot. All went well for a few more days and I thought the antidepressant was settling in. I had to cut a piece of timber for some repairs to a cupboard in our bedroom. I consider myself a good chippie – my old man taught me loads of things constructive when I was a kid and he especially took time to teach me to cut timber or metal dead straight, (less wastage) so I was a dab hand at cutting completely straight and square. Well! Five attempts later and with five bits of badly cut timber on the floor and there I am having a fucking row with myself, when Carol appeared at the doorway to see what all the commotion was. As she came into the bedroom she said, 'John, who the hell are you rowing with?' I was so frustrated that I somehow blamed her for all the fuck-ups on the floor, for asking me to repair the cupboard at a time when I had a lot of stress and worry on my mind.

I had started using excuses like that to justify me going off to the pub. They were a complete load of bollocks and I knew Carol knew it as well, but to be honest, she was just glad some days to see the back end of me and just agree to keep me sweet. The truth here was that I just could not adapt to the Island way of life or the people, I was finding it difficult to maintain a happy-go-lucky attitude. I realise now, that this was when I started to people please, especially with Carol.

I took the 'wonder drug' for a few more days and I was having all sorts of crazy thoughts, that life was great and hunky dory, when in fact my life was fucking shit and I was drinking even more, so I binned the fucking things and my thinking today is that antidepressants are a bad drug and should only be prescribed to people that really have a mental illness and not handed out like fucking sweets by the quacks who can't be bothered to spend an extra bit of time with you to try and find the root of your problem. It's, 'Oh, you're drinking too much because you're unhappy, so take these mind fucking altering drugs and you will be fine, bye, bye.' In all that diagnosis would take five minutes and these fuckers are on 100k per year and call themselves professionals.

We worked the cleaning business sunrise to sunset, nice in the summer but fucking bitter and miserable in the winter and if it rained we were fucked because we couldn't clean windows in that type of weather. My little touch I had with the steroids was dwindling fast and most of it went over the bar. I decided to up my cash flow by going commercial, hotels and offices, which should bring in more income. I went through the phone book and sold myself to all these companies. I was surprised at how much work I got and things began to improve, that is, until I rolled out of the pub one night after being on the piss for eight hours and straight into the arms of our local police patrol. That was my next lesson with learning about these Islanders – they loved grassing on people, especially if you came from the mainland. I was four and a half times over the legal driving limit and in all fairness and honesty I deserved to go to prison. I was even warned by the landlord of the local to walk home because old bill were floating about but I never took a blind bit of notice.

While waiting for my court appearance, there was an arson attack on one of the so-called hard men that lived on the top floor flat opposite me on the estate. It was early evening, about seven and some bright spark decided to set fire to a discarded sofa and two chairs right outside the local hard-man's flat. There was another flat opposite the hard man's, which housed a family of six and the burning sofa and chairs were situated on the top landing between the two flats, which were about four metres apart and most important of all was that the front door was the only means of escape.

I had just finished work and had a few pints around the pub before coming home. I always had a bath every night and was in the process of undressing, when I happened to glance at the block opposite and saw thick black smoke billowing out of both top floor flats, the kind that sinks before rising. The hard man's place seemed to be unoccupied because there were no lights on and no one at the windows, unlike the flat next door. Every window was opened and there were adults and kids shouting for help.

The sofa and chairs which were on fire had formed a thick toxic black smoke which was being sucked under and through the gap of the front door and letter box because all their windows had been opened; this created a wind vacuum affect. The whole top landing was ablaze with flames and putrid smoke, stopping anyone escaping via the front door and the only alternative was to jump fifty feet.

At that particular time our local firemen were called out to deal with several big hotel fires on other parts of the Island and were unable to respond to this emergency. After five minutes, I could see the smoke billowing out of all the windows and the kids were now getting frantic with screams and yelling The fucking locals thought it was the best entertainment they had ever seen and the cowardly wankers even brought out their fucking chairs and carry-outs so they could be more comfortable and have a drink, while watching a whole family about to be burnt to death. You now know why I could not get on with these fucking people, because this lot didn't give a monkey's toss about anyone except themselves.

I put my jeans on and left my tee shirt and ran down the stairs to my van as fast as I could and grabbed the two sets of ladders I had on my truck. I knew that using only one ladder would not be enough to reach the people trapped because of their length, so I tied the two sets together. As I was struggling to carry the ladders to the opposite block, I could see these fuckers gathering at the base of the block and were laughing and joking, I screamed with blind rage at theses fucking red necks, 'For fuck's sake, you bunch of wankers, one of you give me a fucking hand with these fucking ladders.' I was so angry at this point that I even considered beating the fuck out of any one of them before trying to save the family.

A half pissed Irish geezer came running towards me and fell flat on his chin as he reached me, but give credit where it's due, he did get back up and helped me get the ladder up to the window. It was a sickening sight because the ladders, even though they were tied together, still left me five feet short of the window sill.

I shouted up to a geezer who was leaning out of the window, 'The ladder's short! You will have to climb out and slide down until your feet touch the top rung on the ladder.'

His reply was, 'What?' they should have named this geezer 'three times' because after that many times of repeating myself, I just thought 'deaf fucker' then I shouted up, 'Just stay there, I'm coming up.'

His answer to that was – you guessed it. 'What?'

I just mumbled, 'Bollocks,' and in frustration I shouted at the paddy to put his can of special brew down and stand on the foot of the ladder and to hold it in place while I climbed up. As I got to the top of the ladder, I soon realised that I would have to do a balancing act and try and stand on the last rung and hold on to the window sill. Once I got hold of the sill, my head was just about level with the bottom of the outward opening window, the smoke was now as thick as pea soup and the fumes were lethal.

'Right, how many of you?' I shouted.

He shouted back that there were six of them.

I said, 'Pass out the smallest,' thinking he would pass a kid down to me, but no! This geezer passes me a fucking sheep dog. I'm left there holding this dog and I shouted back at the bloke, 'the fucking kids, you idiot, not the dog, what's wrong with you? Pass down the youngest kid to me, quickly, now!'

I shouted down to paddy at the foot of the ladder, 'Catch,' and dropped the sheepdog right on top of him. He went flying when the dog landed on him. Fortunately the dog just got up and ran off okay. However the paddy was not so lucky because he thought he had broken his neck and was moaning like a fucking kid, I then realised that the Irishman hadn't spilt a drop of his beer and just told him to stop moaning and hold on to the ladder. The next thing that was handed to me, was what I thought was a bundle of clothes and I was just about to aim the bundle to the ground in frustration, when I heard a distinctive whimper and then a soft cry of a youngster, I then carefully unravelled the bundle and looked nervously inside and saw a newly born baby and lowered the bundle down to waist level.

'Fuck me!' I said with utter shock and it dawned on me that I nearly threw this kid fifty feet to the ground thinking it was a load of dirty washing. My heart was pounding now and I could not feel my bare feet because of the cold and I was shit scared standing there balancing on the top rung with a young baby in my arms. I prayed to God that I would not slip or fall with the kid then I safely manoeuvred my way down the ladder rungs and handed the kid to the paddy, then quickly returned to the top.

I said to the geezer inside the flat 'Pass the next one down' by this time, the outside area had filled with more onlookers and I noticed an unmarked police car parked up with two old bill inside opposite the block. I had recognised both of them from previous dealings with the boys in blue. I shouted at them to give me some help and then anxiously asked them where the fuck was the fire brigade? One of them shouts from the car window that the fire crews were on their way and that; they could not help me because of insurance reasons. I just flipped when I heard that line of pathetic bullshit and yelled back, 'well you two pair of gutless arseholes should fuck off then, because you're presence here isn't worth a fucking toss.' He mumbled some crap but it fell on deaf ears because in my opinion, if he was a decent caring man, including the other coward that was sitting next to him, between them they could have helped and saved lives, but instead they sat warmly snuggled up with each other watching me struggle to rescue this family.

What happened next was, I saw a big fat arse lowering itself out of the window and it belonged to a seventeen stone thirteen-year-old nipper and as he manoeuvred himself on to the top rung of the ladder, he stands right on the tips of my fingers, I let out a yell and told him to move his feet but keep holding on to the window sill. He seemed shit scared of the height and my flimsy concocted ladder. I managed to come up behind him with both my hands either side of him holding on to the window sill, just to give him the reassurance that I was there and all would be okay only if he followed my instructions. His father had been holding the window open for him to allow him to get out unhindered.

I said to the kid, 'You have to trust me kid and let go of the sill, you're going to be alright son,' before I could say another word, the window came crashing into the back of my head, the force of the blow to my skull nearly sent me hurtling backwards, but somehow I managed to get a firmer grip of the sill just in time. I angrily shouted at the father, 'Not you! You dopey fucking idiot, it's him I want to let go.' The Father kept apologising and was getting himself in a fucking mess. I did feel for him as I explained, 'Look mate, all will be okay, buddy, I promise you that you will all be okay, just do exactly as I say, do you understand?'

He solemnly answered, 'Yes, Mister, please just get my family out.'

I assured him yet again and reminded him that we were running out of time because the smoke was now affecting everyone including me and I was on the outside. I managed to get them all out safe and sound and as the last one set foot on terra firma from the ladder, the fire brigade turned up with sirens blaring and lights flashing.

Five minutes later the ambulance crew arrived and gave us all oxygen because of smoke inhalation, but what I pissed myself laughing at was the fucking cheek of the paddy getting some as well, the fucker was fifty feet below and outside with his can of beer and the only smoke he breathed in was from his own fag. Once I had been cleared by the ambulance crew, I noticed the two old bill had decided to show their mugs from their nice warm car and were talking to the fire crew. One of them noticed me staring at him and called me over. I only had my jeans on, no shirt and was numb from head to toe from the cold; I just gave him a disgraceful look and started walking towards our flat. The same scum bags that were enjoying watching the fire in their deck chairs with their carry-outs decided to come around me and began patting me on the back, telling me that I was a hero and a saver of lives and all that bollocks.

I was still fucking angry with them as they patted me on the back, I shrugged them off and told them to all fuck off and called them all cowards! I was that angry, my gob run away with itself and what flowed was obscene and disgusting language, just as well it was only my gob when I think about it today because if I had, had the energy, I would have probably beaten and battered half a dozen of them, but saving six people and a dog in mid-winter had taken its toll out of me and I was too bloody knackered to kick off, just as well for them.

I ignored the old bill that had waved me over and went straight upstairs to our flat and had a well-earned hot bath to try to get some feeling back into my body. Carol came into the bathroom and gave me a big kiss and called me her hero. I blush very easily and hated the idea of being called a hero or a life saver; I thanked her and said, 'I'm no one's hero sweetheart. I just did what I did on pure instinct, that's all, so please no more hero stuff, you know it embarrasses me.' She gave me a sweet smile and left the bathroom to answer the front door and to be honest secretly I was well chuffed with what she just said calling me her hero, but only her!

As I'm getting out of the bath, with the door on the jar, I noticed the two old bill who had been in their car walk past the bathroom door, down my passageway towards my front room with Carol quickly walking behind them, she gave me 'the look' as she passed me – the look' is a face we would pull at each other only when old bill were about. We never ever trusted the police because when I was being regularly stitched up by them at court, I would look at Carol as I was being led away to the cells, so we adopted this look; every time we came across them and I suppose it became a habit.

I'm now in the front room with the two policemen who had just watched me struggle to save the family. I was still bloody angry as well as hurting inside, this pair of pricks had already made themselves all comfy in 'my spot' on the sofa – everyone has a favourite chair or seat that they sit in and theses two cheeky bastards took my spot, so I told them abruptly to move, which they did, only now they had to stand which suited me fine, considering they had just had front row seats, I reckoned they needed to stretch their legs.

They began to talk to me in their patronising way then came all the 'sorry's… and the 'if only we could have…I'm sure there was a violinist in the fucking corner of the room because these two could have gone on stage, they were that good. I just sat there with a can of beer pretending to listen to this pair of cowards but said nothing. It must have been half an hour before I actually took any notice of what they were saying because after two minutes I just turned off and thought about pie and mash and green liquor, a cockney delicacy, plus a few other things, just to block-out their tiresome bullshit. Then the senior one mentioned a bravery award, my ears became wide open now and I started to listen to what he was saying.

He said, 'Johnny, I am going to personally recommend you for a bravery award. What you did out there was an act of heroism and by having no thought for your own safety, you courageously saved the lives of a family of six. What do you say to that Johnny?'

I replied sarcastically, 'Give me a minute mate, I think my head is about to explode' and I got up from the sofa and went into the kitchen to get another beer. At the same time I could feel my ego was beginning to rise inside me, I thought hero, yeah, that sounds quite good, then bravery award, yeah that's even better. In between me getting the beer out of the fridge and me going back into the room, thank fuck my gut feeling came in and clarity of the whole situation came into focus and my ego was promptly kicked into touch and deflated it pronto

'Well, John, what do think of that buddy?'

I answered with a very serious, no-nonsense look on my face. 'First of all you aren't my buddy and second, the only reason you want to butter me up with all this bravery award and hero bollocks is to keep me sweet, just in case Mr. Journalist comes knocking on my door and I might voice my opinions about you two, am I correct?'

'No John, you got it wrong, I meant what I said about insurance and we would not officially be able to help, just in case'

I replied sharply, 'Just in case of what?'

His partner butted in and said, 'That if one member of that family had died while we were assisting, then we could be sued.'

I just fell back into the chair and took a huge swig from my can, I shouted out to Carol who was with the kids in the bedroom – even my kids never trusted the Police because they had witnessed for themselves in London their old man getting the shit kicked out of him while handcuffed with guns pointed at his head. No wonder they never trusted them and Carol had to hide them away when they were in the house. I said loudly, so she could hear me from the front room, 'they couldn't help me out over there sweetheart, because they were afraid of being sued, did you hear that babe?'

Carol came to the foot of the door and gave these two pricks a piece of her own mind, which I might add was none too clean and as she was speaking, I saw my kids hiding behind her except my eldest daughter Lynsey – she was more inclined to want to belt the fuckers, she takes after me for that I'm afraid. After Carol had said what she thought about their lame excuses, they had realised that their bullshitting patter was not working with us so they started making their way to the front door.

I followed behind and mentioned the bravery award to them; they both replied that they were, even if I did not want one, going to still recommend me for one and if you know the old bill as well as I did back then, then you'll know what I'm about to say – Bravery award my arse, those pair of sleaze bags never put me forward for anything, you know why? Because I am Johnny Mack, the same Johnny Mack who was told a few years earlier after smothering the Island with counterfeit bank notes, which I quite rightly went to prison for, was told that if I ever came to live on the Island, that they would make my life hell and you know what, they did a marvellous job but more of that later.

The next morning was like being raided by old bill, but only this time it was the press. After the old bill had left the night before and Carol and the kids went to bed, I stayed up and drank at least ten cans of strong lager, thinking over what had happened that night, it took ten to make me sleepy. So there I am with a fucking hang-over from hell and a mouth like a Scotchman's jock strap being told by a Gary Bushel look-alike that I'm a HERO! I just slammed the door shut, for fuck sake I've only had two hours kip, the next minute he's shouting kiss ass verbal through the letter box, which woke the kids up, so I let him in and told him to give me five minutes. Instead of getting a cup of tea I went straight to the fridge and downed a can in seconds, gave it five minutes to work then went in to where he was. The kids were all at the doorway listening in, they were quite proud that their Dad was being called a hero and I could hear them saying, 'Dad's going to be famous, he is going to be in the papers.' Ironically I have been in the papers many times, but never for good reasons, but the kids never knew about those occasions.

Anyway this reporter was like a record going at seventy-eight speed, I never got a chance to talk much because as soon as I started to answer his question he would fire another at me. He was gone in fifteen minutes and to be honest I didn't quite know what I had said to him, basically because I was still half-pissed from the night before, it tends to do that when you drink the way I did then.

So we had not been that long on the estate and already, I was building a reputation, one was I was a hero and the other was 'Don't sell him a cooker' – to be honest the way I performed that night of the fire by yelling at all those wankers, made them all a bit wary of me because when my temper came into play everyone would just disappear. I didn't mind the reputation bit because people tended to leave me and my family alone and I was fine with that, after all I was over here on the Island to change my way of life and to start a new beginning wasn't I? It was a nightmare for me living on the rock and believe me when I say I felt like a fish out of water. I just could not get through to the islanders nor could I understand their logic. Remember, I was brought up not to trust anyone outside Peckham and I was finding it so hard to fit in. Getting work was like winning the lottery, all because I was a cockney or an 'overner', as they like to call you. I remember one old boy in our local who fucking hated me, he would always tell me that I'd never be a 'Caulk head' – that's what you were called if you were born and bred on the Island.

In London if I walked up to someone in the area where I was brought up and said, 'Hello, I'm a Caulk head!' I'd either be holding up a flyover or shot through the fucking nut, so that old boy was right, I would never be a called a Caulk head – well all I can say to that is, 'Thank fuck for that?'

# III

# "Plastic Gangsters"?...

I went to court for the drink drive offence and expected to lose my license. What worried me was – for how long? I never bothered with a brief because the ones I saw loitering about the foyer outside the Court looked like they slept in their suits or they had had a night under a bus shelter.

So I went it alone and declined legal assistance. There were three magistrates in all, two men and one woman and believe me when I say they were not a happy bunch. They just stared down at me as if I was a low life or some other form of scum.

The old bill stepped into the witness box to give his evidence. 'We stopped the defendant and approached his van. Once there, we opened the driver's door, the defendant fell onto the road, obviously due to excessive drinking. Once breathalysed he was arrested and taken to the police station, the defendant was further breathalysed with our new Hi-Tech machine and a blood test later revealed a reading of 480 milligrams.' I had no idea what 480 milligrams meant really, but the fucking magistrates seemed to know and all three were now up and listening intently to the cozzer in the box.

I now realised that it wouldn't be how long I could lose my license for, but it was now looking like how long the fuckers were going to bang me up. My brain went into overdrive now, because there was no way I was going down for a muggy drink and drive conviction – how fucking embarrassing, I'd never live it down. When it came to my turn to speak, I asked the bench if I could speak from the witness box and place my hand on the Bible and swear on oath what I had to say. They agreed to my request and in the box I went and said I swear by almighty God etc and started my spill.

I was and still am a very good talker and can at times manipulate people. I am able to a degree to suss people out very quickly as well, so I checked the three beaks out behind the bench and picked one; that would be the one I would concentrate on to give my patter to. From my vast experience I knew how the courts work, for fuck's sake me and courts are like a busman's holiday, I've been in so many all over the country. There's only a few I haven't been in. I started my spill to the chosen beak and laid it on the line and I was only half-way through before she was nearly in tears.

One of the other beaks was just staring into space as if he already made up his mind, so I thought, fuck it! I'll use the hero stuff to see if I could get his attention. Just by chance I happened to have a copy of the local rag, picturing me as a hero saving the lives of a family of six and I asked the bench if they would consider reading the article, to prove that I could be a responsible person, sometimes.

I watched intently at each one as it was passed along; seeing their reactions and facial movements gave me an idea what effect the article was having on them. When the last one had finished reading the press cutting, I piped up and said, 'Your worships, I know now that I was a very selfish and uncaring person the night I drove under the influence and I deserve the harshest of punishments that the law permits, but I can only assure the court that it will never happen again and I would like the court to take into consideration that I can be a useful member of society.'

They took their recess to consider what was to happen to me and after fifteen minutes they reconvened and asked me to rise, I stood upright with my hands behind my back (fingers crossed) and looked right at them. The main beak started going on about that it was the highest blood reading they had came across in the Island courts and for that reason I should be made an example to warn others, straight away. I'm thinking this fucking shopkeeper hasn't taken a blind bit of notice of what I have shown him or said when the woman cut in with her very upper crust voice. She went on to say that because of my heroics, they were not going to send me to prison, but they were considering a three year ban. Then the third one starts to sentence me and says to me eighteen months driving ban and two hundred quid costs.

I came out of there relieved and was chuffed at only getting an eighteen month ban. I did feel a bit guilty about using the hero stuff to save my own arse, but let's be fair, why not use it if it helps me, after all what goes round comes round. I helped that family – now they were helping me without them even knowing it.

I tried to maintain the cleaning business by hiring a driver, but there was not enough money to keep us all going, so I sold the round, the truck, the ladders and all the equipment. I was gutted really and started drinking even more heavily. I convinced myself that if I went to the pub as much as possible then, sooner or later, I would bump into someone who would have some work or put me on to an earner. I had done most of my business in pubs when I lived in Peckham and I thought it would work here on the Island. Where I'd use the pub most of the day and night, I got to know all the locals and after a while I came across one particular character, who I found out later to be a dealer, not class A drugs, just a puff salesman (cannabis) and I ended up round his house one evening having my first joint in a long time.

It felt like heaven once I had had a few tokes on a joint. I felt relaxed for once and ended up falling asleep. I awoke in the early hours and took my puff, which I bought earlier and made my way home. First thing I done was wake Carol to give her a spliff; she was always partial to the odd joint or two, especially in the morning. I went on to tell her that I had started to meet new people, who were partially on my wave length and that maybe we might have an earner coming our way if I get to know this guy and his cronies a bit better. That was partly true, but I was people-pleasing her if I'm to be honest. I was giving her false hope because I desperately wanted her to know that I was trying to provide for my family but I just could not do it on the Island like I could back in back in Peckham. Of course, it also gave me a good reason to be in the pub all the time – complete crap thinking. My drinking had doubled from the time I tried to stop before and I restarted again with a vengeance and near on doubled the amount from what I used to drink.

After a few months without my driving license, we began to feel the effects and our financial situation was at crisis point, yet somehow I still managed to find money for my drink. I had convinced myself that my drinking was acceptable to my family, even when opening a can at seven in the morning, while the kids had their cereal – even doing that did not register with me that I might have an out of control drink problem. You see, I beat my near on fatal skag and crack cocaine addictions with no help from any doctor, rehab or medication and I felt the pain of withdrawal and once clean I thought there was fuck all else out there that could get me hooked. Having a drink problem was the last thing on my mind; after all I had worked with tramps and dossers when I was serving a Borstal sentence when I was a nipper. They called it a C.S.V. (community service volunteer) and those people drank meths and cheap cider all the time and smelt like shit. It was those sorts of people who I classed as alcoholic or had severe drink problems, not me. I only drank this much because I was living on the Isle of Wight, I was skint and I was stressed and as soon as a good earner came along everything would be hunky dory – that's what my thinking was like at that time. It was never my fault, always someone else's.

After getting to know this dealer for a while, I began to understand how things worked, regarding anything dodgy. I was introduced to a few people who I just knew were at it! Most of those I met were younger than me and small fry. And to be honest they were so easy to manipulate and use, so I did just that. And what a fucking big mistake that turned into. I had started buying in dodgy gear from a family of burglars. Their so-called ring leader was their mother called Sue, who was a fat arse of a snaky bitch who got her own sons, plus a fourteen-year-old foster girl who the social services entrusted into this bitch's clutches, to rob pre-picked houses. I had been doing business with her for a while and knew little of how she was getting her merchandise. Only later did I become aware of that. She was one tight-fisted old dog, who took the lion's share of any payment and then paid the family of thieves a pittance for their ill gotten gains and they accepted what they got from the hag without argument. Because she had brain-washed her little team and fed them line upon line of bullshit and promises, they swallowed every bit of it and did her bidding.

Sue always tried to give me a hard time when we were doing business. Everything she brought to me was always of good quality, but I was not a greedy fat pig like her, so she would push and push to get the best price she could get out of me. I needed her because she was at that time my only source of income at that time but I never let her know that. On my last ever dealing with her, it was just a week or two before Christmas, when she came to see me with a beautiful full set of what I will call, 'merchandise'. She thought she knew its true worth, because it was the first time I had seen the fat bitch smile. She walked into my lock-up with the box of 'merchandise' under her arm. I knew she was here for business and pulled down the shutter so we had more privacy and before I could ask or even look at what she had, she said, 'Seven grand, London boy.'

I said to her, 'For fuck's sake, Sue! Let's have a butchers at the stuff before you start demanding how much you want, okay?'

'I am not taking a penny less,' she said.

I said fuck all as I opened up the box and instantly I said to her, 'Nice merchandise, Sue,' then I went on to examine the goods. And as I'm having a good look at the stuff she almost shouts, 'Seven grand, okay?' I just roared at her now and said, 'Why don't you let the fuckers in Portsmouth know about how much you want? Keep your fucking voice down, will ya?' Sue hesitated for a second or two and reached for her inhaler and took a big gulp from it and started to mellow a bit – seeing that showed me what greed does to some people.

I said to her after she got her breath back, 'Look, Sue, I agree with you, it is worth seven grand. But that depends on the merchandise history, for instance, was it taken locally? Or are the people who owned it famous or well known publicly? And is there any chance it might be on the local news or turn up on crime-watch in three months' time? All these things affect the sale price sweetheart.' I said all this in a calm, patronising voice. She went on to give me a story of where the gear came from and that it was kosher and would not be missed for three months because it was taken from a holiday home and the owners were in Bermuda.

I said, 'Give me two hours and I'll bell you after I talk to my man.'

She said, 'Fine,' and gave me a snaky grin and left the lock up.

I was on the phone as soon as Sue left to a pal of mine who was right into this sort of merchandise. I gave him all the info and he gave me an estimated price, bearing in mind he had not even seen the stuff.

'Twelve grand, if it's what you say it is and it is a complete set.'

I knew my man would have this merchandise out of the country in a matter of hours of buying it, straight into the arms of an international collector and it would be sat on for two or three years, then it would pop up in an auction place in Monaco or someplace like that, with a complete false history. The previous owners would not be looking for it as they would have been paid out by the insurers and the insurers would have to spend a lot of legal money to disprove the history this merchandise had acquired in the last few years and that's how the scam works. But you need a lot of patience, good contacts and a wad of cash to make it pay.

I contacted the horrible bitch and agreed a meeting that evening. She turned up with her fat fuck of a son, who called himself 'Rat'. That's the Island for you, who in their right mind would call themselves 'Rat'? Haven't they ever heard that song by UB40 *Rat in the Kitchen* or the film star James Cagney say, 'You dirty rat'? That's what I could never understand about some of the Islanders, the names they would call themselves. If I was living in London and I was introduced to a geezer called 'Rat' I'd probably stab the fucker in the eye, thinking he was a wrong'en with a name like that, surely you can't be trusted.

So rat boy came along with his hag of a mother. When I first saw him, the likeness was unbelievable; from behind you could not tell the difference, but from the front the only difference was the beard and moustache and that was attached to, her face. You have probably gathered I have a great dislike for this woman and soon all will be revealed. When they came in to my lock-up, the son shut the door and Sue says, 'Well, what's the score Johnny?'

I said with the *'best that I can do'* face on, 'Four and a half grand, that's the best I can do for you Sue and that's based on the history you supplied me,' which I knew was all bollocks anyway, that stuff was red hot and the fat bitch knew it all along.

You can shove that price right up your arse Johnny Mack, that's a piss-take,' she shouted.

I said calmly in a sarcastic tone, 'Bye, bye Sue, let yourselves out, only I got a lot on today, know what I mean, sweetheart?'

'Fuck you, too,' was the reply and that's exactly how I knew she would react. Sue was trying to work me, but I was having none of it. I knew I had the advantage because she could not take that stuff to anyone local for the simple reason that she would be grassed up by the plastic criminal element on this Island. It was common practice to grass and still is. She knew if she sold local, then she was taking a big risk, so I was her only hope.

All this 'fuck you' nonsense was play-act on her behalf and that's where she never knew me, she had no idea I had been brought up on the streets and could read most people like Paul McKenna. As they were leaving, she gave me a West Indian kiss jibe 'Ras clat'. I just ignored her and smiled, knowing what was going to happen next. Fuck me! If it took more than five minutes, then I'll be lying. In she came and said, 'Five grand and that's my limit.'

I purposely took a minute to answer her and told her that I would think about it overnight, which I knew really would piss her off, because now it was my time to play-act. The next morning I got up extra early knowing I had to call Sue and I needed a couple of hours to get my head straight be able to deal with her. After three cans I was just about feeling normal and hospitable; all this was before anyone in the house had got up, yet I still never thought that I had a serious drink problem developing and progressively getting worse; to me this was normal behaviour.

I rang Sue just after the kids went to school and arranged a meet at the lock-up in the afternoon as I had a bit of other business to deal with first, so I could not make it sooner, it was all bollocks really. The reason for the later meet was quite simple, opening time was due and I could have a few hours in the pub 'just in case I might meet someone with an earner for me' and I went on to tell my Carol the same, all Walter Mitty bullshit. Later that afternoon I went to meet Sue, who was now on her own waiting impatiently at the lock-up, plus I was an hour late, on purpose of course – after all I was playing her at her own game of play-acting wasn't I.

I made my apologies and let her in, but even before I could turn the light on, she was on my case. I said to her, 'Slow down, Sue, for fuck's sake. You're not even giving me the bloody time to put the kettle on, so sit down and take a fucking breath and then we will get down to business after I've got a cuppa on the go, okay?' She swaggered over to my big captain's chair which was opposite my desk and flopped right into it. 'Crack' was the next sound I heard, and as I turned towards Sue to see what had happened, all I saw was what I thought was a big fat hairy rat with a tail between a pair of tree trunk legs as she went flying across the room and landed on two porcelain figurines worth about seventy five quid each in auction.

I went over and picked her up and helped her on to the sofa, she was using her inhaler as I was summing up the damage the bitch had just done. After she got her breath back, she made a comment about my rickety old chair and how unsafe it was. I half laughed and explained 'That rat that flew up between your legs caused you and all thirty fucking stone of you, to fall back and break a pucker antique captain's chair, which to my reckoning would fetch three hundred quid at any auction and that's not including the two Doulton figurines you crushed as well, that's another one and a half.' She went on to say some load of bollocks, but I shut her up straight away and said, 'you're not doing very well, are you, Sue? So far you owe me for the chair and the figurines and we still haven't settled on a price for your merchandise.' I was in full play-act mode now and I put my 'don't fuck with me serious face on as I knelt in front of her. She was sitting opened-legged; that on its own was nearly enough for me to puke my guts up. 'Listen, Sue, I got you your five grand and that's without me getting a drink out of it, so I was hoping you would give me at least a monkey (£500) for moving the stuff, but now you already owe me nearly that amount for the stuff you've broke, plus my drink for moving it, so make up your mind, or pay me for what you broke, okay?'

She was about to start up again, but I noticed she was working hard not to, that's when I knew I had her. A few more puffs on her inhaler with a self pitying look on her face and she replied quite calmly, 'Four and half and we are quits, you okay with that, John?'

'Sure, Sue, no problem, I'm more than happy with that arrangement, but what about my broken goods?'

She came back sharply and said, 'You're a piss taker Johnny Mack will three hundred quid keep you sweet?' I paused for a short moment then agreed.

I collected and paid Sue money for the 'merchandise' the next morning – it was gone in under five hours and day, it probably ended up in some European antique dealer's collection by the next.

Sue came to visit me a few times after that last bit of business, with all sorts of gear. Some of it was 'very nice' and a good earner could have been made. I had a problem with Sue and her gear and that was now down to 'Morals' – to cut a long story short, I had them, but that evil bitch had none. I had recently become aware through a sound acquaintance of mine how Sue had been obtaining her merchandise, as

I've already mentioned it came through the kids and that was against my code of practice – I felt like Fagin, for fuck's sake.

I did my best to keep quiet and not let my opinion or my big mouth have its say, but ten cans and half a bottle of brandy later, half the fucking Island knew. That's how fucked up I was, my thinking was totally negative and all over the bloody place and if I'm honest, I hated her and everyone associated with her, if she had been a geezer, then I think that I would have probably half-killed her, because using kids to do the dirty work is out of order in my book. I now know Sue heard about my rants and raves about her and you and we all know about the saying *Be warned a woman scorned* well, only now I was about to learn a valuable lesson, and that was to feel the full brunt of the bitch.

# IV

# "Bonnie and Clyde"

Carol and the kids had started putting up all the Christmas decorations in our flat and you could feel the buzz oozing from the kids and of course Carol, who was more like a big kid herself at that time of year and as I understand it, still is. Dad's job was the tree, and the extortionate prices that were being asked were daylight robbery. This was when I knew that I was not working on all six cylinders.

I had been brought up with infamous villains, from an infamous area; I was taught loyalty, trust and especially how not to be a mug. My whole criminal education was 'how not to get caught' be smart, never grass and never rob your own.

There I am in a massive forest area at nine in the evening, cutting down a thirty five foot Christmas tree. The height of my ceiling was eight foot, so I had gathered that I may have to lose a foot or two. I cut and dragged that fucking tree at least two hundred yards, laid it next to the truck and cut a few feet off. That was the easy bit, the hard bit was trying to get the tree on the truck, it must have weighed a ton, I'm a strong geezer and I only just managed to get the base of the trunk on to the back of the truck, effing and blinding quietly to myself, when I heard this voice come from the shadows of the surrounding trees and this geezer appears from nowhere. I'm stood there with this fucking tree, thinking this is all I need; I've been rumbled, for nicking a poxy Christmas tree. My mind projected to what our local paper would say – 'Hero steals protected tree' – but more importantly, my kids would be gutted as I had promised them the best and biggest tree in the world and Dads always keep their promises, don't they?

I don't know how, nor do I wish to know, why what happened next, the geezer says to me, 'You must be Vic the Bear? My name is Larry. I'm sorry I was not here to meet you on time, only I could not get the forklift to work, but its fine now, so let me load the tree on the wagon for you.'

I quickly summed up what was going on and just said, 'I did wait, but ended up taking it myself. I thought you may have had a problem, so I just carried on, I hope that's okay with you?'

He just said, 'No problem Vic you wait there and I'll bring the fork lift round.' He loaded the tree on and even helped me tie it down. I thanked the geezer and slipped him a fiver, which he was over the moon with, but I'm thinking what the fuck's going on here and just drove off with him waving me on and wishing me a happy Christmas.

It was obvious I was mistaken for someone else, but to actually start to play-act when I thought I was nicked paid off.

Well, by the time I arrived home the kids were all waiting to see what the tree was like that Dad was bringing home. They had been boasting to their mates that their Dad was getting the best tree ever, so there were a quite a few of my kids friends waiting with them at the foot of our flats. Well the picture on their faces was priceless, when they saw the size of it as I pulled into the estate, their friends were opened-mouthed and my Carol was pissing herself with laughter as she was looking out of the window. The tree was three times longer than the truck and as I had been driving it, it had cleaned half the streets I had driven home on because there was everything from tin cans to a dead cat tangled in amongst the end of the tree. Well, we did have a marvellous tree, so did four of our neighbours' after I had cut it up. It's at this point I would like to thank 'Vic the Bear', whoever you are, because you made quite a few people happy. I just hope that Larry never got into too much trouble, because he was a very nice geezer and ever so helpful. The next morning I was abruptly awoken by a familiar phrase that I had heard many times before when living in Peckham.

'Armed Police if you Move, you horrible bastard, you will end up a dead man,' that came from one of the officers of our special tactical firearms unit who had his sub machine gun pressed so fucking hard against my temple that it left an impression for over a week, then I was jumped on, punched in the kidneys and half strangled while being handcuffed and was then pulled out of bed and dragged upright. I was completely naked as was my Carol who was trying to hide her dignity with the bed quilt with a room full of armed police.

I screamed at the bastards to give Carol some privacy or let her put something on and screamed even louder at the wankers for waving their loaded firearms around in the air in the corridor which was only four foot wide and twelve foot long with my three kids screaming their heads off. To be honest, I've had the best of the metropolitan police robbery squad (The Sweeney) come and arrest me with their arsenal of weapons, but not once did I have to go mad at their tactics, they knew how to handle me, women and kids in these sorts of situations. In other words, they had a tried and tested plan whereby no one, especially a kid, could get scared or hurt – they were professionals and I still have respect for the bastards today.

But this bunch was more likely to be at home in the Wild West and was acting like fucking amateurs; they were a danger not only to my Carol and the kids, but to themselves as well. They acted as if they had a part in a Carry On film. They dragged me to the front door with just a pair of jeans pulled half way up, so my bollocks and arse were on full show for all to see. At my front door I came face to face with a detective sergeant who had a grey handlebar moustache carrying a four foot water pipe in his hand. I said, 'So what do you think you are, then? A fucking Water Board inspector with that in your hand?' I had to laugh at this joker because he said to his crony, 'Book him, Danno,' just like in the Hawaii five 0 TV detective series. Then they dragged me down the stairs across the car park, with my jeans now around my ankles and it was fucking freezing, my poor todger looked like a shrivelled prune. I was screaming every obscenity I could muster at them, for fuck's sake, they had not even told me what I was getting nicked for, let alone read me my rights. They put me in the middle of two fat old bill in the back of their car and the RAF. Look-alike water-board prick was sitting in the front with his lucky water pipe between his legs.

I asked the prick, 'Well, Biggle's what the fuck, are you nicking me for?' He turned his head half way in my direction and said, 'We finally got you now, Johnny boy, and it's looking more like a fifteen stretch for you.'

I shouted, 'What the fuck is this, a million questions or something? What am I bloody nicked for?'

'Armed robbery,' was his reply.

My heart felt like it was about to shoot out of my arse when he said that, I was well taken back and went completely silent because of shock.

I knew from my old school teachings not to say a fucking word until I had seen a brief especially when armed robbery was mentioned. There was one brief I used, called Graham, who worked for a firm of solicitors in the Ryde area of the Island and he only dealt with crime. I had and still have a lot of respect for the geezer. He is straight as a dye and that's saying something considering he was a scouser, (comes from Liverpool) but the most important and staunch thing about the geezer was that, if he thought you were innocent, then he would fight hand over fist for you. If your crime took you to Crown Court, then he would try his hardest to get the best Counsel or even a Queen's Counsel to defend you, he was that genuine.

I'm dragged out of the police car at the rear of Shanklin police station and taken into the charge room, where they pushed me up against the wall for another body search and to see if I had concealed a gun or a fucking rocket-propelled grenade launcher up my arse, then the sergeant who was sitting behind his huge counter desk asked me if I'm happy with the treatment I have received since being arrested.

I ask you! What a fucking ridiculous stupid question to ask me, after the way they had just performed, so I said to the sergeant, 'Well that depends on this fucker searching me because if his finger slips I don't think I'll be a very happy bunny.'

He said straight away, 'Prisoner declined to answer, no reply.' I was used to all these fucking stupid mind games, I had probably been in more of these scenarios then they have so I would just let the pricks get on with it. In fact, they made very good entertainment, especially when it came to their interrogation tactics'. I had dealings with this police force before when I was nicked for distributing counterfeit twenty pound notes and spreading a few thousand on the Island – the Courts said it was wrong, but I said, 'I thought that I was helping the economy out.' But they never saw it my way and gave me a few years to think it over.

I'm dragged, still handcuffed, down to the cell area to the furthest cell which turned out to be their top security cell; in other words it had two doors, one being solid with a square hatch and the other being a door of bars. There I was, freezing my arse off, with just a pair of jeans only half way on; you could see my breath when I breathed out, because it was that fucking cold. So, considering I knew their routine as I have just explained, I knew the bastards would have been up early that morning and after they have arrested their target and got him banged up in one of their minus ten star en suite rooms, they would go and stuff their fat faces with greasy canteen food, then after they had had their grub it would be interrogation time, that was their usual routine for dawn raids.

As I was slightly pissed off, freezing and starving, I decided to jog round the cell to get the circulation flowing, I decided to start shouting at the top of my voice, knowing that the acoustics of the cell would treble the sound of my rants and piss them off big time 'Feed me you cunts!' is how I started, then as I repeated the line over and over again, I got louder and louder until a wide arse woman sergeant appeared at the hatch really pissed off with a face like thunder. She roared at me as if I was a naughty school boy

'Keep your noise down and I will fetch you something to eat ok?'

I said, 'Okay and fetch me some blankets as well, because I'm frozen.'

About ten minutes later she's at the hatch with a cheese burger in a plastic box. 'Here you go' she said as she passed it through the hatch.

I went over to the hatch and said, It would help if you removed these fucking handcuffs,' and turned to show her my hands.

The silly bitch says, 'Wait there and I will get the key.'

I said sarcastically, 'Wait here? Where else do you think I'm going? To a football match?' The burger landed at my feet, obviously aimed at me and off she marched, squeak' squeak' was the sound that came from her Doc Martens rubber footwear as she stormed up the concrete floored corridor.

About an hour later, the 'A team' arrived at my cell along with the R.A.F. wing commander water board so called detective sergeant hiding behind them, one of them opens my cell doors up, they rush at me and pin me to the floor. They removed my jeans for forensics then took the cuffs off and backed out of the cell one by one, leaving the last one holding me down so he could make a bolt for the cell door, before I could get to my feet and kick off at them.

The burger was stone cold and I was stark naked and as cold as *jack frost*, so I thought out loudly, 'Okay you bastards, let's give you fuckers a bit more agro, only this time, a real piece of your own medicine, considering your treating me like an animal, then I shall act like one'. I binned the cold burger down the toilet and held the plastic container wide open and squatted, then very precisely shit in the box area. I then went to the cell door, where they had kindly left the sliding hatch open. I put my whole arm through with the box of shit and then went on to smear the door handle and all the surrounding area with shit.

It took less than ten minutes, before I got the reaction I had been hoping for. There was a lot of commotion outside my cell; I heard some of them puking up their lovely fried breakfasts and the others were calling me an animal and all sorts. I had put myself right out of sight by squatting on top of the toilet seat which was in an alcove and completely out of sight from the cell door while they were all arguing who was going to clear the mess, let alone get me out for interrogation because the door lock was full of shit. I sat squatted on the toilet shouting at the fuckers and telling them that I have another turd waiting for the first one that came through the door, I then went into graphic detail on how I was going to make him eat it. My objective had worked; they got something they never expected when they nicked me, trouble'.

By this time I didn't give a fuck anymore so I kept winding them up to come in. 'Come on!' I shouted. 'What's up boys? Frightened of a bit of shit, are we?'

They were going ape shit outside and that made me feel quite good in a mad sort of way even though my whole body was numb from the cold, I started to laugh and as I got louder, they must have thought I was a complete nutter. The next thing that happened took me by surprise; I thought the water board DC really was working in the water industry because the bastards steamed in real quick and sprayed me with a high pressure hose.

Already numb from the cold and having a high pressure hose used on you nearly brings on hyperthermia and then you're fucked, well I was. I just rolled up in a ball and protected what was left of my poor shrivelled-up bollocks, waiting for the kicking. Instead three blankets were thrown at me and a lighted cigarette and then the door and hatch were slammed shut. I quickly got up and grabbed the blankets because I was shaking like a rampant rabbit, a girl's best friend. Taking that first drag on that fag was like heaven and I could feel the stress subside, just like my first drink of the day. I smoked that fag down to the filter and got myself partially warm with the aid of the blankets and just sat on the concrete floor there and waited for their next move. Well I never had to wait that long before the wing commander opens the hatch and calls me over to the door for a chat, on a promise of a phone call to my brief.

I got to my feet and walked over to the door, with the blankets draped around me with soaking wet hair, I must have looked liked *Charlton Heston* out of the film *Ben Hurr*. I said to him as I reached the door, 'Where's my wife?' He took a step back from the hatch and said with the biggest of grins I have had ever seen on a geezer and said with sick minded intent, 'We nicked your Missus and your kids have all been taken into care.' Then he calmly walked away laughing.

My reaction was manic, 'You fucking low life piece of shit, let her go! Please, let her go.' That bastard laughed even louder when he heard the word 'please' come from my lips.

I stopped shouting the place down and calmed down, mainly due to exhaustion, I decided to wait and see what was next on their agenda because I was now more worried for Carol and the kids then me and the bastards were now playing mind games especially with that knowledge. My thinking was different now and this nightmare had to be sorted out quickly for the sakes of Carol and the kids, not mine. All this was the norm to me; I had been in this situation many times before, so I was used to it, but they changed the rules and played dirty by using Carol and the kids as pawns and that's where they had me. About an hour later, a uniformed cozzer came to the door and said, 'Mack you got one phone call, come with me and no trouble okay?' I answered 'That's the last thing on my mind' as he unlocked the cell. I was put on the phone to my brief and he updated me on my situation. For instance, they were accusing Carol and me of an armed robbery at Ventnor town post office. Carol was, in the Old Bills' eyes, my getaway driver and I was the blagger (robber). I instantly felt relief, because this was one of those rare occasions when I knew I was completely innocent, let alone Carol. She couldn't even fucking drive a Tesco trolley, let alone be a getaway driver!

I asked my brief to get over as soon as possible and he said that he would be with me once he had sorted Carol out. I said, 'Where have the fuckers got her, Graham?'

He replied, 'Newport police station, John.'

'What about the kids? These bastards have told me they are in foster care.'

Graham was brilliant at calming me down, because he knew me very well and if left to my own devices in a room full of old bill, then it was highly likely all hell could break loose. 'Calm down, John, the kids are safe at home with a social worker, they are not thinking of putting the kids in care.'

He asked me how I wanted to handle the situation regarding the interrogation as it would be sometime before he could get to me, I gave a wild stare at the police that were in the room with me and told him, 'I'm happy to go this one alone as I'm about to make these bunch of dirty wankers!' Suddenly, the phone was pulled out of my hand and I was again dragged screaming back to my cell. It was obvious the old bill didn't agree with my opinion of them and here's me thinking – 'what happened to freedom of speech' as I'm thrown back into the cell.

About half hour later, the wing commander came and spoke to me out of sight of the hatch; he probably thought I had another turd waiting for him. 'Want a chat, John?' he said from behind the wall.

'Fucking right, I do!' I shouted as I put my head into the hatch leaving my ears wedged on each side. 'Where the fuck are you then?' I screamed.

The slippery git answers 'I'm right here, Johnny, but if we can chat on a civil level, then I can soon see us sorting all this out very quickly, what do you think Johnny?' Then he appeared from behind the wall and handed me another lighted fag.

I was up for getting all this sorted, as I did know I was innocent and I had not done a blag for some time, so in my eyes the truth prevails. So we sat down for the interrogation – as I said earlier, I did not need a brief on this one really because as I said I was completely innocent and apart from that I had been in this situation many times before, so I knew how it worked and knew what to say and do.

The Wing Commander started the interrogation with dates and times over the last week; well I was mostly pissed throughout the time he had mentioned and I couldn't even remember everything I had done yesterday, let alone a week ago. Usually my memory was always very good; well I thought it was, until I was being interrogated this time. You have to be careful when you answer any questions when you're under caution, everything you say is evidence and if you start changing your story due to simple forgetfulness, the prosecution has this uncanny way of making you out to be a fucking liar, by you not giving the correct answer in the first place. I only answered those questions that I could be absolutely sure were truthful, the rest were answered with a 'No comment' which would give me more time to try and remember.

Then he mentioned a certain date, which I remembered very well and it was only a few days ago. He asked me where I had been between nine in the morning and one in the afternoon. I replied, 'At nine o'clock, I was at the dentist in Ryde having treatment and that went on till ten thirty. I then went on to Ryde boxing club to train an up and coming boxer called Jason Primmer, (who went on to become a pro) and trained with him until one thirty in the afternoon.' The cozzer stops the interrogation and returns me to my cell. It was obvious that the date and times mentioned were when the blag occurred and my alibi was telling him that I was in a dentist chair with plenty of witnesses and the boxing club where Jason could back me up, you would think I had nothing to worry about. While sitting in the cell, I was convinced that they must know that they had the wrong man and that they would let me go with an apology. After an hour, the Wing Commander came for me to continue the interrogation. I thought, 'here we go again John Boy', he was now trying a new tactic which I thought, was trying to keep me sweet, because he must now know, that they had fucked up big time, now they have checked out my alibis and would now do their best to sweet talk me so I didn't make a complaint against them. Well, fucking how wrong was I, here's me, thinking, I'll be home in an hour.

He asked me, 'How fit are you, John?'

I asked him, 'Why?'

'Just answer the question,' was his reply.

Now at that time I was boxing training a nipper who had a lot of potential, so we trained six days a week, so I was quite fit and we would do four and a half miles of road work most days except Sundays. Thinking back now, that I was able to train and run distances gave me a false sense of reality – 'how could I have a drink problem when I train the way I do?' I had been conning myself that I was okay. 'Pretty fit, I suppose,' was my reply.

'Do you jog?' he asked.

'Yes, I do, what's all this got to do with this blag?'

'All in good time, my dear boy, and all will be explained. Now, where's your car?' he asked.

I was just loving this prick ask me pathetic questions because I really thought he was wasting time to give himself an excuse to let me go without him making himself look a mug. So I went along with it, but this idiot either had a huge ego problem and would not admit defeat, or he was a scum bag of a stitch-up merchant and did not give a fuck who got nicked as long as he got the credit for the nicking – well it turned out he was the latter. Bent police are the scum of the earth; they destroy people's lives, families and the character of the innocent, just so long as they get their fucking brownie points and maybe a promotion and this fucker and his DCI were of that calibre.

I told this scumbag, 'I don't have a car.'

He said, 'What about the wife?'

I told him, 'She does not own, nor can she drive, a car.'

Then he went on to tell me this amazing fairy story of what he thought had happened. His brilliant detective analyst convinced him that because I had trained at the boxing club near on daily for over a year, he somehow thought in his own strange world, that I was a super fit blagger, faster than an Olympic gold medallist or the Six Million Dollar Man and with that assumption he believed that I robbed the post office at nine in the morning and then ran from Ventnor to the dentist in Ryde – which is about fifteen miles – and arrived at the dentist at nine fifteen without an ounce of sweat dripping and stashed the dough along the way. I was speechless for once in my life and looked at this idiot with amazement and shock and finally said to him, 'Do you know anything of maths? Have you really considered what you are actually saying?' He just looked at me real smug-like sitting and leaning forward on his lucky water pipe. I went on to explain the math's of me running fifteen miles across open country in fifteen minutes.

It had no effect on him and he just sat smirking at me, then the door opens and another cozzer brings in two plastic evidence bags with what looked like a toy gun inside one and in the other a white powder then he hands them to the Wing Commander. His eyes lit up like a Christmas tree. 'Well, well, what do we have here then Macky-boy?

I said, 'Let's have a look then?' he then hands me a see-through bag. Inside was what looked like a toy gun, not like the replicated ones of today, it looked more like a *Mickey Mouse* gun that fired plastic sticks with suckers on the end and if you pointed that thing at anyone I should think they would roll over on the floor laughing, it was that ridiculous. I asked the Wing Commander, 'Where did that antique toy come from?'

The other cozzer piped up and says, 'But John, it's yours.'

I said, 'What the fuck are you talking about? I've never seen that in my life, is that the best you can do you pair of amateurs?'

The Wing Commander then throws the other small opened plastic bag containing a white crystal powder on to the table, then tells me in his own slimy way, 'Not only armed robbery now, but class A drug dealing me old china, that little lot should make your sentence a roundabout figure of fifteen years or more.'

I just about had enough of their fucking stupid mind games and jumped up from the table, pushing the chair back and shouted, 'See that plastic bag of powder? That came from my kitchen and it was in a box, which you purposely removed and on that fucking box, it says 'wine bottle bleach crystals' which for your information means it's not a fucking class A drug, so get your drug testing kit on it and stop wasting my fucking time, in fact, fuck you! Take me back to my cell and get my brief, otherwise, we don't do anymore talking.'

He just nodded at the uniformed cozzer in the room to get me back to the cell block because I reckon he was thinking that he was coming close to a right-hander and believe me I was seriously considering it. It was now Christmas Eve, I had still not seen my brief and as far as I was concerned, these bent cozzers were planning on charging me with armed robbery, plus Class A drug dealing. It would be obvious that they would have to open up a special court because of the festive season and of course the time, as it was late afternoon and the format for the police at court would be to just simply ask the Magistrate for a remand in custody for a month so they can gather their forensic and other non-existing evidence. So I needed Graham, my brief. I rang the cell bell and kicked fuck out of the door and screamed to piss them off. It was shortly after, that I heard Graham's voice just outside my cell and he was not too happy with the way the police were handling my case.

They eventually let him into my cell and closed the door behind him. The first thing I asked him was, 'How's my Carol? What have the bastards done to her?' As I said before, Graham could calm me down and he explained that Carol was now at home and the kids were okay, the relief that came over me was enough to put me asleep. You see from experience, I expected to spend Christmas and the New Year in custody on remand in Winchester prison, even though I was completely innocent; the courts always took notice of the old bill rather than the defendant when they were applying for bail and that's the way the system has worked for years, all that innocent until proven guilty was all pie in the sky bullshit because they already had you an custody. There, I would be held until they came back with their anticipated fabricated forensic evidence; it was normal procedure at that time. No magistrate would give me bail, especially with my past convictions, so I started telling Graham to get my radio and deodorant, toothpaste and of course baccy, all the stuff I would need if things went pear-shaped at court. Graham had got quite shitty with the police and mentioned that he had been waiting over three hours to see me and the reason the old bill gave to prevent him from seeing me was that they feared for his own personal safety as I was acting like an animal (Saucy bastards).

Graham takes a lot to get wound up, He knew the delaying tactics they would use, but he must have said or done the right thing because he got in to see me. He knew they were trying to delay our meeting for as long as possible. He said, 'John, we have to get you bail, they have no evidence on you at all. They should have released you a long time ago.'

I said, 'Okay, Graham, what do we do now?'

He said, 'Don't give them any more shit, verbal or the real thing, okay?' he said, with a smirk on his face. 'And I will sort the Court out, okay, John?'

I said, 'Okay, mate, thanks for all you're doing for Carol and me, but don't forget the list I gave you. You know, just in case it doesn't work out.' Bless him he wrote it all down and left.

It was seven in the evening when they came for me, They gave me some light clothing to put on to make me look half presentable to the court and then they handcuffed me from behind and marched me into a van with six old bill, some armed. I thought they were going over the top with this charade, but that was only half of it, they had me in a centre of what I believe was a convoy with police cars and motor cycles with their sirens blaring and their lights flashing as escorts; you'd have thought that they had captured Ronnie Biggs or Freddie Foreman.

Once at the court I was taken into the holding cell before being brought before the magistrate and there must have been six old bill and four prison officers keeping an eye on me locked in a cage. Talk about a fucking waste of tax payers money and even today I personally feel our penal system and the way it is presented is nothing more than a sham and a scam. The police are the worse culprits – how many applications for legal aid are granted to people who have been arrested and charged by the Police who have little or no evidence? I'll tell you, shall I? Fucking thousands and the price for a brief back then was £150 per hour let alone the letter scam; take my advice, never write to a solicitor because it will cost you £40 for a fucking reply and that's probably their trainee who wrote it. So the system stinks and that's my honest opinion.

Graham stuck his head into my cage and said with a big grin and a bit of banter 'Want a banana?' I had to laugh at his wit with me sitting in a fucking cage, he went on to tell me more seriously 'John, we have a fair magistrate sitting on the bench alone' I knew from experience the workings of the various ranks of the bench which would make that magistrate a stipendiary and not just the normal lay ones, these stipendiary ones would generally be lawyers or work in the field of law whereas the lay magistrates were nothing more than shopkeepers and businessmen or women and had limited knowledge of Law. They worked in threes and would mainly rely on the court clerk for their direction and these ones mostly leant in the Police's favour, especially when they were giving their evidence. Basically, it would almost be guaranteed a Christmas bang up if I was in front of the lays, whereas now I stood a chance with the other one – bad timing, for the old bill that is.

There I was in the dock at a Newport magistrates' Court at eight pm on Christmas Eve with a prison officer each side, armed police behind. I sat there, listening to this so called professional policeman with the rank of Detective inspector explain to the bench what a dangerous man I was and went on to give his 'expert knowledge' of the bleaching powder and 'toy gun' and from his huge experience he went on to explain to the bench that the substance was a class A drug and the toy gun was a possible firearm.

I sat with my head in my hands listening to this complete load of verbal diarrhoea coming from a so called respected Detective Inspector. Then it was the Wing Commander's turn to enter the witness box. He never said that much but was stumped with the question when he was asked about me running fifteen miles in fifteen minutes, He hesitated and could not give a satisfactory answer and to be honest what with that and Graham's speech I got bail.

Graham, as I said, was a straight lawyer and would fight for you if you were innocent and I was quite taken back at what his finishing speech to the bench was. He stood upright with his hands in a clenched prayer-like clasp in front of him and said, 'Ma'am, I have practiced in this Court and on this Island for the last twelve years and in all that time, I have never come across a case where there is absolutely no evidence, my client has the perfect alibi, in fact he has three, yet I am hearing a complete heap-full of non-factual evidence coming from those officers who have just given evidence and I ask you to grant my client bail, until the police gather their so called forensic evidence and be one hundred percent sure before it being presented to this court.' Well now my head was up and looking around at everyone, especially the old bird on the bench. She was a big build of a woman, a bit like *Hattie Jacques*, the actress in the *Carry On films* and she was writing notes. I looked at the Wing Commander and he could not make eye contact with me at all, in fact none of the shameful bastards could.

The magistrate asked the DI to enter the witness box again and asked him what qualifications he had in forensic science? There was a moment of silence, and then he replied, 'None, Ma'am.' Then she asked how he thought it was possible for me the defendant to complete the miles mentioned in world record time? This time the dodgy bugger had slaughtered himself because he said a good 'running' friend had given him the information and that this friend had told him that it was possible.

Well, the whole court could all see that the magistrate was getting slightly pissed off with him and stopped the questioning half way through then said these words that were music to my ears. 'I have heard all I need.' Then she went on to say, 'Bail will be granted on condition the defendant signs at the police station every day at a time agreed.'

I just felt this enormous amount of relief come over me and I could have just laid down and slept. I was, by this time mentally fucked, yet there was worse to come. I eventually arrived home at eleven in the evening and the flat was completely wrecked; just seeing my Carol broke my heart because she was in complete shock. The kids were wondering what was going on and were asking me a million questions and as all this was going on, I looked around the living room and noticed that the Christmas tree was leaning at an angle, with lots of ripped present wrapping all sprawled over the floor around the tree. I raised my hand and stopped everyone from asking me questions and walked over to the tree to straighten it and to see where the paper had come from.

I think you will now understand why I have been so anti-police throughout my story. What I saw, once the tree had been put upright, was all of the kids' Christmas presents, which had been laid out all nice and neatly prior to when the burglars' arrived, had been ripped open and emptied on the floor and just left where they had been dropped, some had been walked on and crushed and others had been pulled apart and just discarded on the floor. My eldest daughter, Lynsey, explained to me that the police had made them all except their mother, who was in Newport Police station, sit on the sofa all day while they opened all their presents and pulled them apart right in front of them and then blatantly threw them on the deck. Not only did they do that, they ate from our fridge because they had pulled our flat apart bit by bit which took them near on all day, so the lazy fuckers helped themselves to our food instead of getting their own and then the cheeky bastards ate our food right in front of my kids and it sickens me to say that they never even offered them anything. What sort of people could do that in front of young children – well the Isle of Wight Police thought they could, and did.

I went to put some warm clothing on, only to find that the bastards had taken every scrap of clothing I possessed for forensic testing, including my underwear, shoes and even my socks. They also took all our money, what little we had at that time and the bastards even drank most of my beer from the fridge. I felt completely gutted and useless. I was completely broken-hearted for my Carol and the kids. My parents helped the best they could and even brought me a few beers round. My parents knew I had been a villain in the past and probably thought I deserved all I got, but I have never complained or felt sorry for myself when caught for something I was guilty for, which meant, I never put upon them when I got myself banged up. To me that went with my chosen profession, but this time they knew I was innocent and realised I was being stitched up because one of my alibis was that, my parents had been talking to me at my flat just before I went to the dentist on the morning of the blag and it was obvious the police took no notice of her and that had a big impact on my mother because she always presumed that the police were straight as a dye. Unfortunately she adapted a different opinion after what she had witnessed

As I said earlier, my memory was not that clever due to the booze, I had no recollection of that conversation with my parents that morning. Today I realise that this was the start of what I now know was my alcoholism beginning to show its symptoms, the booze had started to work against me – in other words, this illness was beginning to take over my life because the booze had stopped working for me, whereas before it gave me confidence, a good sense of wellbeing and the ability to deal with situations, places and people, but now things were slowly going downhill and I could not understand why these changes were happening to me.

Carol had started telling me what they had done with her while she was in custody. She told me that they were so convincing with their spiel that even she had doubts that maybe, 'I had done the robbery'. To be honest, I had always kept Carol out of any illegal dealings I had always done in the past, as far as she knew, I was a villain but she never asked me questions, so she knew fuck all, that's why the Metropolitan Police would never bother her – what could she tell them? Nothing! No decent crook involves the mother of his kids in his business – anyway it's safer that way, just in case they divorce you and try and blackmail you later in life.

Carol went on to tell me how she was treated by these so-called, 'protectors of the public. I was really gutted when she tearfully told me the only clothing she was allowed to wear was an old green maternity dress, she had no underwear or footwear and what with all the shock she was being put through, those bastards did not notice that she was having a miscarriage in her cell, and to top it all she had to near on beg a civilian cell block cleaner for a tampon, because she thought she was having a heavy period, unaware she was pregnant. All the cleaner could muster was a sanitary towel. Poor Carol had no underwear to hold that in place, so not only did they humiliate and embarrass her, they destroyed what confidence she had with the police.

They took her dignity, pride and every moral fibre out of her while they had her in their custody, they were fucking animals treating her the way they did and when it was all explained to me I remember going into the bathroom and crying my eyes out in frustration because in my mind, all of this trouble had been caused by me, all because I'm *Johnny Mack* who had an infamous reputation which he brought to the Island from Peckham. My heart went out to Carol that Christmas Eve, she is a very strong woman and is straight as a dye and a brilliant mum, but those bastards broke her and as you can gather, I still hate those fucker's involved till this day for what they did to her.

My parents had said that the police had turned their place over and found a toy gun, mum went on to tell me that she confiscated it from me when I was four years of age for getting up to mischief and it was left in a box which she had kept untouched for years, being as she was a hoarder, no wonder I never recognised it when they showed it to me. My mother told me that she had told them of our conversation we had before I went to the dentist, so not one nor two but I had three alibis, just goes to show you how wrong our justice systems was at that time. The ironic thing about this robbery was, five years later I spoke to a geezer who had either been present or knew someone who had been at the post office that morning of the raid and it was said that the cashier recognised the robber by his 'voice even though he had a mask on and the Hampshire so-called elite police force knew of that as well, so why did the bastards put my Carol, my kids and my elderly parents and me through that ordeal when they already fucking knew who had done it. I'll tell you why they did what they did to me, shall I? Apart from my reputation, Fat Sue, the Fagin of the Island decided to inform the old bill with false information about me. The greedy bitch wanted to claim the reward and grassed me. I was already warned not to move here and as I have already mentioned they promised to make my life hell if I did, well I did move here and they kept to their word true to form and succeeded with the aid of that horrible bitch.

The old bill eventually caught the pair who had done the blag and copped for them coming back from Spain after spending all their ill gotten gains, but did my family and I get an apology? Did we fuck, accept six trips to the police station to try and get our money and belongings back and that took six weeks. Graham my brief contacted me after the charges were dropped to tell me I had a very good case to sue the bastards especially the way we had all been treated, but where I was brought up in Peckham, if we sued the old bill then word would be put about the ranks and my life would have been made hell, they would've had a field day nicking me for everything and anything, but I decided not to because there was no way of us knowing if these fuckers would be of the same calibre as the Peckham old bill I carried that anger and guilt for a long time – in some way I felt I had let my family down, even though I was innocent after all. Moving to the Rock was meant to be a new start, not only for me but for Carol and the kids. My past was catching up with me now and I was scared if I'm to be honest and when that fear came I started drinking even more. It just seemed to numb the feelings, anxieties, and fears I was experiencing but when they got worse, I simply drank more to suppress them.

I went to the doctor's several times again because I was getting violent and angry but they just offered me antidepressants again and anger management. I knew what the pills would do to me and wanted none of it. I just wanted answers! Why was it that I had to sometimes drink in the mornings to get straight? Why was it, that I could not make a telephone call without a drink? Why was it that I was getting angry more frequently? No doctor could answer me, so I tried willpower to limit my intake and control my drinking to see if that would work.

I went on to get some sort of order with the drinking by going back to honest work on the building sites, but the majority of building workers were piss heads, so that was a smart move on my behalf. But what it did for me was to help me to give up drinking in the day time, apart from a few days, so I got into this routine whereby I was able to work and deal with people again on an acceptable level. But with anything with self-will involved, it does not last that long. It depends on how strong you are, which determines how long the routine would last.

While it did last for me, I earnt good money, got promoted to contracts manager and ended up overseeing many contracts. Without being too big-headed, I am quite clever and on the ball when sober. I could pull some amazing deals off which brought big bonuses for me and big profits for the company I was working for, and I'm talking legal here. I have to be honest when I say crime does not pay. Well, for me it didn't, I earned more working legally then when I worked the pavement with a shooter or robbing some shit head of a crack dealer.

It carried on that way for a year or so, until the stress of running six or seven contracts at once started me back to drinking every day (all day) so I had a couple of the lads do most of my work, which meant my bonuses would be far less because I had to split it with them. It was mainly paperwork and meetings that they did for me. I always thought that I could multi-task and I did for quite some time, that was until the booze stopped working for me. I thought that this would only be temporary and that I had enough money stashed to cover the loss until I got my head sorted, I couldn't have been more wrong. Carol had her money for the housekeeping and all she needed for the kids, at first she never complained of my drinking, apart from the odd outburst from me, but as I got slowly worse, so did my outbursts, a bit like a see-saw up one minute then down the next. Eventually Carol had to 'work me without me even knowing; she had no choice if she was ever to get a quite life living with me and my drinking, she worked it so as to avoid me losing the plot and causing ructions in the house. It had by then become the norm for me to have a drink in my hand, which meant my mood could change like the weather. I had to wind up some of the contracts because a recession had started to set in and I was owed twenty-eight thousand pounds in bonuses from a main contractor who it turned out had no intention of paying me. I had big problems when trying to get my money from him at first, but with a bit of Peckham persuasion and a temper like the fucking *Hulk* he coughed up and I was able to pay my men off. What money was left never lasted long, mainly down the pub or off-license, then a stroke of luck came our way when we were offered a council housing exchange from the estate we were on to a beautiful village cottage right on the coast.

This was one of our dreams, we had three in all, one was a cottage by the sea with a garden in a select location, the second was owning a boat and the third was a Land Rover, all of which we got in the years ahead, so we were not asking for a lot. Carol never really shared my dreams; unfortunately some of mine were quick fix and usually bollocks because I always wanted everything yesterday, because today was not good enough for me, no fucking patience was my main problem whereby Carol just wanted peace and quiet and to be with the kids. Our little dream gave me the drive to curb my drinking because it seemed it was coming together and when I got the boat, well, I was two thirds there in my mind, but being me I still wanted that Land Rover, yesterday.

I came up with this crazy idea of earning a living from the sea and decided to familiarise myself with the Solent, which was the name of the surrounding waters. I met a young guy called Buddha who offered to look after my new boat while it was moored, in exchange for letting him come out with me to do a spot of fishing, which I did. This geezer, even though he was a teenager had a lot of knowledge of the sea and the surrounding area and he helped me a great deal.

I soon realised from the local fishermen that there was good money in crab and lobster and seeing I now had a somewhat limited knowledge of the waters, I decided to go into the shellfish business and went on to make my own pots. On my first trip out to lay my handmade pots, I needed a hand to string them out or if I tried it on my own I ran the risk of being caught up in the string line and dragged overboard. Buddha was not about at the time, so I took a Cockney geezer called Tim out with me. He had recently moved to the Island and had an over-the-top fascination with Second World War relics, especially if they were German. I'm sure he was a bloody secret Nazi because his favourite chatter always involved fucking Hitler, even if he was talking about a football match, Hitler would always crop up somewhere, I have to admit Tim was an odd ball but a nice geezer. We set off on a clear summer's morning. I bullshitted Tim that I was an expert on navigation, otherwise he wouldn't have come out with me, so we set off in the Solent making our way just past a place called The Nab Tower, which was about nine miles out to sea. The boat was a twenty-two foot open Dory with an outboard engine and the whole boat was stacked shoulder high with pots and of course, plenty of nine percent strength lager. About an hour into our venture, a heavy fog appeared and quickly came down on us, it was as thick as pea soup; lucky for us I noticed a buoy in the shipping lane and headed towards it to moor up until the fog had cleared. After two hours and ten cans later, Tim said, 'I'm getting a bit worried here, Johnny.' Again I bullshitted him not to worry because, as an expert navigator, how could we get lost? To be honest I never had a clue which way land was, let alone where I was. I just gave him more beer until we both passed out.

When we awoke after four hours, the fog was just as bad and Tim kept going on at me to go inshore and back to dry land. I did my best in stalling him but he was now getting worried and inpatient. What he didn't know was, I was getting a bit worried as well and decided to untie the rope on the mooring and take a chance. Tim asked me, 'Where's your compass mate?'

I said quite confidently, 'I don't need one, Tim.'

His face changed to a grey worried look and said, 'Well, how the fuck are you going to get us back through this fog?'

I ignored his question and said, 'Relax Tim, open up another couple of tins will ya and make yourself useful?'

Then I saw fear in Tim's face when he noticed me sticking my finger in my mouth and pointing it in the air – I had seen it done in loads of films. Tim said, 'Is that your fucking compass?'

'Sure is, Tim,' I said as I started the engine and throttled away from the buoy into the fog. The truth was, I never had a bloody clue what direction we were heading in, for all I knew we were on our way to France instead of heading back to the Island. We had been travelling for about an hour and the fog was still bad. I checked the fuel and we had about half a gallon left, so instead of praying, I just opened up another can and made Tim think all was okay and carried on making out that I never had a care in the world. Then the engine began to flutter due to lack of fuel and then nothing! We were adrift, but where? I never had a fucking clue. Tim was going on a bit now and started to panic, when, what I can only describe as a miracle happened, the fog just lifted like a stage curtain and we found ourselves two hundred yards from where we set out from that morning. Tim still tells the story today probably with Hitler in it somewhere and is totally convinced that I am an expert in seamanship to this day, but the truth is, I put his and my own life at risk and that was all down to my drinking and the stinking thinking it produced.

# V

# "Import Duty"

After a few months, the fish business was going well enough to feed us and I was quite enjoying myself out on the ocean waves. I was learning to know my way about in the Solent, by drinking with the local fishermen and young Buddha. These people knew nothing of my shellfish enterprise and had no idea I was laying strings of pots miles out at sea. It took me two months to realise that you had to be registered with the fisheries board. I honestly thought the sea was a free place, but our Government thought differently.

I would only go out before sunrise and come back after sunset, so no one knew what I was up to. I never wanted anyone to know my business as I found it hard to trust anyone on the Island, especially after the Ventnor blag, anyway it wasn't as if I was up to my old tricks back in Peckham and to me that was a vast improvement. I loved the idea of going out at night, some nights it would be Force ten winds and I would still go out knowing the local fishermen were all tucked up in their beds fearing the weather – to be honest, it was fucking madness when I think of it today. I was pissed most of the time and didn't give a fuck for my personal safety. My temper had calmed down a great deal while I was out on the ocean waves, it was what I always wanted, to lose that aggression. Carol and I stopped arguing and fighting with each other and we seemed to be really happy. I had always regretted fighting with my Carol and would apologise profusely after any row, even if it wasn't my fault and the reason was I could never debate and if I had a drink in me, then I could be a complete nightmare and would smash things and lose total control. Having that boat gave me an outlet and when you're out at sea on your own with all the elements, often it makes you think, even when I was pissed out there, I would pray to God to ask him to change me to be a better person. I felt closer to Him out there because of the solitude and I could just have a conversation with Him – it felt like I had a crew mate and was not alone.

On one particular night, I was on my way back with enough fish for our supper when I saw one of the cross Channel ferries all lit up coming along the shipping lane from France. I would never have my lights on as I preferred not to be seen, so I moved away from the break water they make, as the swell from these ships can capsize your boat very easily, especially one like mine. I had some lucky escapes out there on the waves, for instance, I got so pissed one night I completely blacked out and just as I came round a fucking huge tanker was nearly on top of me – thank fuck for my crew mate because I believe today it was Him that woke me up.

Anyway, getting back to my return journey, I was about two hundred yards off the side of the ferry and was just drifting looking at all the people I could clearly see sitting inside the ship and those who were wandering about on deck, wondering where they had been, did they enjoy themselves? Which part of France did they go to? It was just my imagination really and in a way I envied them because my personal dream was to travel once all the kids had grown up and left, after all I had my first born when I was seventeen and I dreamt of travelling the world when I would be in my prime.

As the ferry passed me, I saw what looked like a rolled carpet fall from the stern of the ship and hit the water with a splash. I immediately stood up to get a better view, when there was another splash, then another. I concentrated on the spot where the splashes were as the ferry was getting further away and I noticed some movement in the water. In fact, it was three people with life jackets on. I instantly thought these people were in trouble and started the engine and made my way over to their location. Once I reached them, I noticed they were all Asian and they started climbing aboard and as I helped them on board they started trying to kiss and hug me, they were so excited and were jabbering on in a foreign language to each other. Now I might not be the brightest person, but it took me all of a minute to realise that these fuckers were illegals and I was not meant to pick them up, so who was? I told the fuckers to stop shouting and laughing by getting my fish knife out and in sign language put the blade to my throat and drew my finger across my lips and said 'Shush!' Instantly they all froze. They had the look of fear in their eyes, I'm not surprised with my ugly menacing face and a gutting knife in my hand, the poor bastards probably thought I was going to kill them, until I said, 'It's okay,' over and over again then they just sat huddled together looking at each other.

I was now thinking, what the fuck am I to do with these geezers, then I heard a boat engine in the distance and it was going full throttle and getting louder as it approached me. I could not see it as it had no lights on, so I panicked a bit and started throwing my catch over the side thinking it was the Coastguard or the fucking Navy. The boat came closer and closer and the sound of the engine was now deafening, but I could not see a bloody thing apart from three sets of pearly white teeth belonging to the three natives. I thought it must be customs because that's their game, rounding up illegals or so I thought, and then wham! My boat was rammed and span it three sixty degrees, then there was a single spot light on us, I could see fuck-all except shadows behind the spot light.

I went into play-act mode thinking they were official. I started shouting my mouth off at them, 'What the fuck do you think you're doing you bastards?' as the boat circled us with its light on us all the time. I'm standing on deck with knife in hand and doing a balancing act at the same time because of the swell coming from their craft. They cut their engine and turned their spot light off and turned torches on, I then saw it wasn't the fucking Customs or the Navy. A voice I recognised said, 'Is that you, Johnny?'

I said, 'Yeah, it's fucking me, what the fuck, are you playing at?'

A rope was thrown over to me and I pulled our two boats together. I could see more clearly now and saw three geezers, all of whom I knew, especially the one with the mouth. He jumped on board my boat and said, 'I see you have picked up our cargo,' as he looked at the three Asians.

I said, 'Your cargo? It looks like your cargo belongs to me now.'

He replied with a kiss ass voice, 'What makes you think that, John?'

I knew the score now and put together what these fuckers were up to, so I replied, 'Salvage.'

He just looked at his crew and they just shrugged their shoulders as if to say, don't ask us. He said, 'Look, John, these guys have to be on shore in fifteen minutes, otherwise certain people will be incredibly pissed off and I don't want to be the one to tell them that you have nicked their cargo.'

I now moved within a few feet of him with knife in hand and said, 'Are you threatening me by chance?' He said, 'I am just stating a fact Johnny. It will be out of my hands if I return empty-handed and they will be none too pleased with you.'

That was it for me. He just went way over my principles regarding giving my name to people I did not know and as far as I was concerned he was threatening me by grassing and I hate grasses, so I grabbed him by the throat and put the knife under his chin and said, 'Look, you cunt, you have no idea who or what I'm about. I was not born here, matey, I only live here, you wanker, and you just broke my code of conduct, so what's stopping me from sticking this blade in your fucking head and throwing your corpse over the side?'

His face changed to a frightened little boy and he replied, 'Look, John, it's all down to bad timing, we had no idea you were out here and we don't want any trouble okay?'

I angrily replied, 'Trouble! You wanker, you ram my boat, make me throw the best catch I have ever had over the side and then you got the front to tell me I might upset people, what sort of cunt do you think I am, eh? Anyway, if it weren't for me these poor fuckers would have been taken with the current and ended up in Southampton dead. What have you got to say about that? Say it with one word.'

He just froze and stared at me briefly, then said, 'Compensation.'

'Correct answer,' I said. We spoke briefly regarding how much I would get and I passed the Asian geezers over to them and just as they were getting on board his boat they shook my hand and bowed and managed to say thank you. We had made an arrangement to meet the next day for my compensation and as he was leaving I said, 'Don't be late, will ya? Otherwise I'll come looking for you, understand?'

He just grunted a 'yep'. And considering we were living on the rock it would not be too hard to find him if he decided to avoid me, apart from that I had come upon a nice little earner this night and was quite pleased with myself and made my way back inshore.

I learnt something that night, which made me form a certain respect for the criminal element on the Island, because it was dawning on me that this was not Peckham and things here were worked differently.

A few days later, there were weather reports of a big storm brewing off the coast and that meant getting my boat on shore. Buddha came into my house as the storm hit, to warn me that I would have trouble getting my boat on to dry land if I did not act quickly. I was well oiled by then and reassured him the boat would be okay, because I had laid an extra mooring block and fitted an extra automatic pump, but Buddha just said, 'John, that will make no difference, this is a big one.'

I thanked him for his advice and went back to my, now favourite pastime, drinking, and as I have already mentioned, when I'm pissed, my thinking is bollocks and I can't be told. The next morning the storm had passed and it was bright and sunny. I wish I could have said that about my head; I had a hangover from hell and needed a livener to get me straight and went over what I could remember from the night before, when it dawned on me what Buddha had warned me, so I decided I would go and check my boat at its mooring.

As I got near to the beach, I noticed a few people coming up the pathway towards me, all of them carrying bits and pieces of marine equipment. It was not until I was right on top of them that I realised the gear they were carrying all belonged to my boat; my heart sank when they told me where they had found the gear. I couldn't even be bothered to ask for my gear back and started running down to the slipway. Once in sight of my mooring, I was stopped dead in my tracks because there was no sign of the boat and as I turned to look up the beach I saw my pride and joy, which had been completely, destroyed lying on the rocks in pieces with all these people milling around it salvaging bits before the tide came in. What did I do? Headed for the pub and got completely pissed and ended up taking my anger out by giving an innocent geezer a good hiding, which resulted in me getting banned from the only pub in the village. Good thinking, eh?

For the next few years I lived to drink and life was a big haze for me. I tried to be a good husband and father by drinking at home alone, most times in another room, so I could be out of everyone's way, so I would not upset them. My thinking just got from bad to worst and I would just sit on the sofa drinking and chain smoking, dreaming that things would get better.

At this time Carol was seeing me go downhill pretty fast and the kids were walking on eggshells around me. I could see uncertainty in the kids' faces when they approached me, especially when they needed my help or wanted a lift to a sports event. I would really try not to drink if they needed a lift, but I let them down nine times out of ten, which made me feel guilty and a fucking useless father, but instead of doing something about it, my answer was, 'Next time kids. I'll be okay because Dad is much stressed and needs a drink today to calm him down.' Their faces were always the same – disappointment. My Carol would have to bullshit other parents to pick up our kids because I never kept my word and the kids would have to be briefed that Dad's car is broken or I was ill, it was all bollocks and the parents knew it, because it carried on like that for years and in a small community it gets noticed. My favourite word was 'Tomorrow' and 'I know' when I tried speaking with Carol about my drinking, it was so hard for me to explain to her what was happening to me. She had seen me come off heroin and crack cocaine with no medical help and stay clean, what she could not get her head round was why I could not stop drinking. My mother noticed a big difference in me when the booze started running my life; after all, she had been born into an alcoholic family in Dublin and had watched her own father drink himself to death in his forties. She also knew all the tricks and traits that alcoholics use.

Time and time again my mum would ask me to stop drinking and I hated her for it. I lied constantly to her to try and get a few bob from her for some tins or a bottle. I thought I was the best liar in the world and that there was no one out there who could tell what I was up to, except Mum. She could read me like a book and even if I was on the phone to her, her first words would be, 'Have you been drinking, son?' before we even had a conversation, She just knew. I created a lot of resentment for Mum's super powers and avoided her for several years. My dad was probably delighted with not seeing me because I had become a pain in the arse and he was fed up to the back teeth with me – all this was down to what the drink had turned me into.

I was desperate for money now and my mind would wander back to my days in Peckham, where I could just walk out of the front door in the morning and nine times out of ten would come back in the evening with an earner, but reality was sinking in and catching up with me fast. I felt completely lost at this stage in my life. I would think that I was putting on a brave face for Carol and the kids, but, if the truth be known, I was fooling no one except myself. It even got to the point that the only way I could sleep, even with a drink down me was to invent scenarios in my head that by chance I would win the lottery or find a boat on the beach which had been used by drug traffickers and a few kilos of cocaine were left aboard, all crazy shit thinking. I really did not want to go thieving again, because here on the Island was not my environment and apart from that, this place had more grasses then Epping Forest, plus most importantly I had promised Carol that I would stay straight, but when you consume large amounts of booze daily, those promises go out, the window along with your thinking.

I foolishly got involved in buying proceeds from crime out of desperation, to sell on and as I had predicted was grassed up, ironically by Fat Sue's son, Rat, and copped eighteen months bird, His nick-name did him proud because along with his mother he was an endless source of information to the local constabulary and the madness in me knew what he was like, yet I still dealt with the fucker, that's where my drinking was taking me.

I was sent to Winchester Prison in Hampshire, I had already done a two year stretch there for the dodgy snide money so I knew the score and after a few weeks in there once the shakes and sweats had subsided, I began to feel so much better. I ended up with my old job as prison barber, which meant I could get into the gym daily and build up on all the weight I had gained from drinking into solid muscle and what with the other perks of the job, I felt contented and safe – sounds ridiculous doesn't it, but I realise today that being banged up was a way of stopping me drinking and if I was not drinking then I was not an asshole to my family.

Carol came regularly to see me with our kids. I knew they could see a difference in me. I started art classes and won an arts award for my work. Mind you, I only ever painted naked women, copying mainly famous works, from artists from the sixteenth and seventeenth centuries. I think it was also that I am an ass man at heart; I do love a woman's butt and seeing I was getting none I decided to paint them instead. After six months of my sentence, I was put in front of a parole board and just told them what they wanted to hear. I was told that I would have to wait for their answer and in the meantime my time at Winchester was about to come to an unscheduled end.

'Bastards,' I shouted at my cell mate as I entered our twelve by six cell with a paper chitty in my hands.

He said, 'What's up with you, Mack?'

I replied, 'The fuckers have de-categorised me from a B to a C and want to send me to the Verne prison, a poxy Cat C nick.'

He just laughed at me and said, 'Mack, I did a four stretch down there, it's a fucking holiday camp, you'll love it especially at this time of year, you will have a holiday maker's tan by the time your jam-roll comes through, so stop your moaning.'

I angrily replied, 'Moaning! I'm fucking entitled to moan, you dumb fuck! Do you realise what this move will do for me apart from a fucking sun tan?'

He just murmured, 'What?'

'I'll tell you what; first of all, I'll lose all my earners, baccy, gear, and the cash that I earn in here and second, how the fuck is my old woman and the kids going to get to that place?'

His reply was quite comical but to the point. 'For fuck's sake, Mack, just take some stock with you, just enough to see you through to your parole and go home with a tan and tell the neighbours' you've been working in Saudi Arabia.'

Well I just paused then saw the funny side and creased up with laughter and just said to him, 'Thanks, mate, I feel better already.'

He said to me, 'You feel better, what about me? You ungrateful, whinging bastard! I've got another fourteen years to do, you have a good think about that Mack before you next start fucking moaning.' And of course, he was right, so I just accepted it.

I saw the gates shut behind the prison van as we left Winchester; it was a real beauty of a sunny day. There were ten of us being shipped out and we were all handcuffed to each other; some were destined for Dorchester prison and the rest of us were destined for Butlins.

When we reached Portland Bill we could see the prison right on top of what looked like a mountain to me and as we drove a spiral route up to the top, there in front of us was what looked like a new nick. I had only ever been in Victorian-built prisons, so the thought of what my cell mate had said came flooding back – holiday camp, sun tan, maybe parole – I felt okay about this nick even before we had driven inside, it had a good feeling about it, mad it might seem, but that's just how I was feeling. As we were being driven to the reception, I noticed a Pitch & Putt course and the cons were playing in just their shorts and guess what? Every fucker had a tan.

Once we had been processed, we were given prison clothing, bedding and a key. I said to the screw, 'What's with the key, Guv?'

He looked at me briefly with his regimental stare then said, 'Well, how the bloody hell do you expect to get into your room without a key, laddie?'

I just looked at him confused; He then went on to explain to me that here at the Verne all cons are given their own key. I thought, fucking hell, this place is home from home and I've even got my own door key. I settled into the induction unit quite well and after a couple of weeks I was put into the main population and boy, did this place look sweet, compared with some of the shit holes I had been in. In the Verne, you were not given a job, you had to go to the employment unit and apply for one, and I suppose it was the system's way of giving us thieving bastards a little knowledge on how to get a job once we were released. Because of my barbering skills, they offered me the hairstylist job, which was a pucker job and it was one that I knew I could work to my advantage, but one thing held me back from taking it, and that was the sunshine and the thought of a tan. I had been banged up for a while now and I was white and pasty looking and after seeing all the other cons looking bronzed, I decided not to take the job because basically it was an inside job which meant no sun, but they gave me seven days to find another or they would give me a job and that meant a real shit one, like peeling spuds or a washer-up.

I went straight to the screw that was in charge of the gardens party and asked for a start. He looked me up and down, and then said in a deep Dorset accent, 'What was your occupation on the outside, Mack?'

Well I had to think fast here because I thought this geezer wanted me to come back with an answer on an agriculture basis and I knew fuck all about plants, but I thought, fuck it, for once tell the truth, as he must have heard all types of bollocks from us cons a million times over and my Cockney accent would make me out to be a liar, so I said, 'Well, Guv, that's a hard one as I have had quite a few, but they were all in the same field.'

He just stared at me, and then said, 'Well?'

I just shrugged my shoulders and said, 'Armed robber, burglar, fraudster, drug dealer and a receiver of stolen goods and I haven't got a clue about gardens, but I'm willing to learn, so give us a job?'

His reply took me back a bit, when he said, 'I have worked this garden party for the best part of twenty years and in all that time, not one of you scum bags has been honest enough to tell me what they were before they came in here.'

Straight away I knew he was putty in my hands, a real softy so I decided to bring a bit of wit into our conversation and said, 'There's more Guv. I use to flog dodgy money…' and before I could finish he stopped me by saying, 'that's enough of your Cockney chit chat, you start Monday, eight sharp and don't be late.' I thought, wait a minute, what the fuck is he talking about don't be late, how the fuck could I be late, I'm in the bloody nick, but that was just how laid back it was, you even had to get yourself up in the morning and put yourself to bed at night, there were no screws coming round and banging (locking) you up at night and no slopping (emptying your chamber pot) out in the mornings, quite cushy really. I realised that this prison held a lot of long-term prisoners who were nearing the end of their sentences and this type of regime was used to ease them back into a routine that would help them when they were released into society.

My wages were three quid per week, which just about covered my baccy and toiletries, but I had a little stash which I had brought from Winchester, which helped when things got tight, so I managed quite well. I loved working in the gardens and I was using my own brand of sun-tan lotion, vinegar and baby oil a factor of 0 and in a few weeks I looked like an Italian and what with the weight training and sports I felt and looked like a new man. Those days of misery brought on by my drinking all day and night were quickly forgotten, I must have thought that I had just been having a run of bad luck which made me drink so much. My brain is the most deceiving thing about me, it can make me feel great, when in fact everything around me is falling to pieces and convinces me that I have not got a problem in the world, then it can send me into a depressive state whereby I would almost drink myself to death, but all the same, that grey matter between my ears would keep telling me to drink more and everything would be okay, complete madness.

After a month on the gardens, I was called to the Assistant Governor's office, where he went on to tell me that my parole had been granted and I would be released within a week. I made my way to the welfare officer who kindly let me use the phone, so I could give Carol and the kids the good news. Carol was over the moon and went on to tell me that she and our kids had arranged to visit the next day. I came away from that phone call elated and had the biggest Cheshire grin on my face; most cons know that look and just say 'parole, nice one.'

I never slept a wink that night and played poker with a few cons, the poor fuckers couldn't read my face through the big grin on my face and so I had the advantage and won quite a bit. I went on to use that expression in future games on the outside and it had the same effect and they say you learn fuck all in jail – well I learnt how to play poker quite successfully.

The visit was very emotional, especially seeing my eldest daughter Lynsey; I had not seen her for what seemed like years, her expression was one of shock and happiness because she was looking at her father who was no longer that drunken fat angry slob. She could see that twinkle back in my eyes and she kept going on about my tan and my weight loss. To be honest, she was always jealous of my ability to get the best suntan out of all our family and I would take full advantage of rubbing it in, by comparing my arm to hers and call her honky in a West Indian dialect which would wind her up rotten. It was all taken in good fun, after all that's what dads do, don't they?

I had been writing regular to Carol telling her that things would be different once I got home, a thing I had done a few times before. I promised I would stop the drinking, get a job and be a good husband

and believe me, I honestly meant every word I wrote. The morning came when I was released and I was led through reception to pick up my civvies clothes and discharge grant, then I was led to the main gate thinking a coach or taxi would be waiting for me to take me to Weymouth railway station, but when the gates slammed shut behind me there was fuck all transport waiting. I did think of knocking on the gates to ask what the fuck were they playing at, but instead I thought, fuck it I'm free and don't want to ask the bastards for anything, so I walked down the spiral road and made my own way, cursing the fuckers every step of the way. By the time I reached the station, my train was already at the platform ready to leave and I just barely made it on board. I started walking the length of the train to find a suitable seat, so the one I decided to pick was in the buffet car, good thinking, hey?

There was no thought of the promises I had made to my wife and kids, my brain was telling me – Johnny Boy! It will be okay this time, you're feeling good, you're just out of stir, so why not just have one drink, you deserve it – and that's exactly what I did. As soon as the first sip of lager touched my lips, the one drink became ten and within an hour I was pissed and blacked out. The guard on the train came round and awoke me before the train set off on its return journey. I felt like I had come out of a bad dream, the feeling of fear, anxiety and disappointment had returned and I was gutted with myself because I knew deep down that I was back to square one.

Carol seemed okay with my return to drinking. I think she just thought that I would be okay and be able to handle it because I had assured her that I had it under control, but the truth was, I had just started where I left off and within a month, I was back at that bench in the kitchen just staring out of the window just supping away, thinking that all would be okay. Everything started to go downhill pretty fast, but I could not see it, except in the mornings when reality had returned. But my answer to all that was going on with me was to drink as quickly as possible because it managed to numb the feelings I should have been feeling. Quite often I would wake in the middle of the night and panic at the thought of not having a drink in the house. You could not get a drink from the off-license until eleven am in the area where I lived, but my thinking was always cautious at running low so I would always manage to buy extra and stash a bottle for just an occasion. The lying and deceiving had returned, because my attitude towards people started to change. I knew I was in deep trouble and tried to pull myself together many times, but always with the same outcome – failure. I started blaming everyone else for my situation, even my parents. Mum could see me going downhill again and nagged me rotten to seek help, but my answer was always the same – Mum, I haven't got a drink problem, I'm just a bit depressed that's all.

There were times when I would even blame Carol for coming to the Island for our problems; I had quickly forgotten that she had probably saved my life by leaving London with the kids. It was that move she made that made me find the strength to get off the drugs because my family meant so much to me; the thought of them being far away from me was not what I wanted. I have said before, family is all I had left and I would do anything for them......except that is, to stop drinking.

Carol had become pregnant with our youngest daughter, Josie-Lee. We had decided that four kids would be enough and Josie would be our last child. I decided to start another window cleaning business and got a loan from the bank. Boy, did I have to work that bank manager. He was hard work because the only collateral I had was my mouth, but by the time I had finished with my spiel to him, he offered me more than I asked for.

We got ladders and a truck and went to work. Carol was only a few months pregnant and she insisted that she was okay to help. If Carol insisted then there was no point in arguing with her, because she is a strong and determined woman. This working partnership between us worked well for the next few months, we would be out in all weathers, so it was fair to say that we worked our arses off to make a living in preparation for our newest family member, Josie. The night came when Carol's waters broke. I was sitting at my bench in the kitchen as usual with a beer in my hand when she entered carrying her maternity bag and said in a calm voice, 'It's time, sweetheart, the ambulance is on it's way.' She was fantastic when it came to childbirth, she had it all sussed out, after all she had already done this three times before and two of them were without me because I was in prison for my eldest Lynsey, working when Frank was born and present at the birth of Danny. I had to stay behind and babysit our three others while Carol gave birth to our beautiful daughter.

I remember going to the hospital the next day with what I could only say was the most expensive bunch of roses ever, I did not have time to complain to the geezer in the shop as I was all over the place with the thought of seeing our newborn daughter. Carol creased up with laughter when I asked the nurse for a vase of water for these expensive flowers.

I said to her, 'what's up with you babe?' but she carried on laughing, then the bird in the next bed did the same. I'm thinking, am I in the right ward here, because most women usually hate their old man after childbirth not start wetting themselves with laughter. The nurse took pity on me and put me right in the end because the bloody flowers I had bought had turned out to be silk – everyone else could tell but not me.

Once Carol and Josie arrived home I knew that the cleaning game was not enough to feed all of us because it was too unreliable. I made contact with some old work mates (legal work) and took on a job erecting air-conditioning. The money was great, but the only drawback was that I had to work away from home. To earn good money back then, you had to go to the mainland for your work because wages on the Island were crap. At first I traveled daily to London which meant being up at four am and not getting back until eight in the evening and believe me I did that routine for several months and it was killing me.

I would make sure I was in bed at ten in the evening which meant I had only two hours for my food and a shower but somehow I still managed to polish off at least two bottles of wine and a few pints of lager and within a short time I was back to normal as one grumpy mother fucker, not only at work but at home as well. I was determined to burn the candle at both ends, which meant my health was beginning to suffer. I could be heard half a mile away coughing my lungs up each morning before the birds were singing, I know that Carol and the kids were burying their heads under their duvets and they would complain non-stop.

I decided to get a bed-sit in Camden Town, North London which was only a tube ride to my place of work in the city. This was much better for me because it meant I could have a couple of more hours in bed and be back at the bed-sit by six in the evening, that was the good side and the bad side was I could now drink three bottles as well as a visit to the local pub each night, another bit of good thinking by me.

I flourished in the job at first and got promoted quickly which meant having quite a few blokes working under me. At first the geezers working with me were great to me and we all got on like a house on fire, but it was not long before my attitude changed for the worse. I overheard a conversation between two of the geezers and they were talking about the 'Reaper, I butted in and asked 'who's the Reaper then?' they became really embarrassed and they started to stutter and mince their words 'Well who's the Reaper' I said. Again there was a silence between them and they were acting like school kids who had just been caught bang to rites when it dawned on me that it was me who they were referring to, I was the reaper. I let the incident go and tried to make fun of the situation just to show face but deep down it had affected me badly and got me thinking that my family probably thought the same about me, after all they would always wave me off when I returned to London on a Sunday after having just spent the weekend at home which was most unusual for my kids, I would always think Ahhhh they're such sweet kids for doing that but I now know different because they were just pleased to see the back end of me.

I arrived back one weekend and just had a big bonus; the kids would always get a handout as soon as I come through the door. Josie, our youngest was always full of energy and wanted all the attention. She had just started walking at this stage and on this occasion she was running about all over the place with excitement, when she made a grab for her blackcurrant drink on the kitchen side, but it turned out to be boiling water in a beaker she would use for her fruit drinks. Carol had put the beaker in soak to remove the stains and unfortunately she had forgotten to tighten the screw top and when Josie made a grab for it the boiling water went partially over one side of her body.

The days that followed were a nightmare for Carol and I, our local hospital were unable to treat Josie so they moved her to the famous Oddstock Hospital in Salisbury and it was there that she underwent plastic surgery. I have to give Carol credit where credit is due. She was a fantastic mum and a very caring parent to all our kids because she never left Josie's side from the time of the accident happening right up until she came back to the Island. We had to make emergency arrangements on how the house was to be run whilst Carol was away at Oddstock. I had to be at work in London or there would have been a good chance I would lose my job, so our eldest daughter Lynsey took control of the family while we were away. She became Mum, Dad, and sister to her two brothers and ran the house fantastically and that was a kid who was only fourteen. My Lynsey went on to make me proud to be her Father and is today still a very caring, loving but shrewd woman.

During that time I cut down on my drinking because I wanted to be on the ball thinking wise, the accident really shook me up and affected me deeply, after all when it's one of your own kids you're seeing in pain, it makes you think how precious they are to you, so I made another attempt at curbing my drinking and did so for a number of years. Our house was argument free for most of that time and my thinking was beginning to alter for the better.

On the job front I ended up taking over a contract I was working on in St Paul's in London's stockbroker area and re-employed all of the geezers that had been working there originally. Good money followed and with that sense of financial security came complacency in my thinking, so my drinking increased and the anxiety and stress returned with a vengeance, much worse than the other times. It brought on fucking weird thoughts in my head, some days I would even contemplate suicide as a way of making everything be okay, but I would have been a gutless arsehole when it came to something like that which tells you something about me. So I decided to try something I hadn't tried for a few years and that was returning to the Church. I was too proud to go to a service or talk to a priest so I opted to go inside the Church when I knew it was empty and in there I would kneel and pray my hardest to a God I believed in but my thinking was that my God never had time for me because I had been quite an evil bastard in my lifetime and I was now receiving a bit of well-earned payback nevertheless I prayed near on every day, but did it stop me drinking... Did it fuck.'

Whilst waiting for a fucking divine bolt of lightning from above to strike me up the arse and change me into the Pope, I carried on the same routine as I had always done in the pass, only this time I tried my hardest not to cause any ructions at home. That's when the lies and bollocks would just come flooding from my lips to Carol, just so I could justify my going down the pub or stay out late drinking, I used every trick in the book, but as I have already said before I was fooling no one except myself.

I had now started up a small construction company mainly doing hard landscaping. It was hard work starting out but I managed to build it up along with a good reputation for giving quality workmanship. The local companies were none too pleased with an 'Overner' doing quite well and they went out of their way to fuck me over by bad mouthing me to customers and in the pub where I drank. I only took their amateur tactics for a short while before they were getting the odd beating from me and that seemed to do the trick and the skullduggery stopped and I was allowed to continue to do my business in peace.

Carol often came working with me especially when someone failed to show for work, as I said before Carol was never one to shy from hard graft and to be honest she was better than some of the locals I employed. I went Limited Company when the business improved and because we had extra cash we decided to buy the house that we had been renting from the council. Carol had been reluctant to give up the tenancy from the local authority, but my argument was that we would be able to leave it to our kids when we popped our clogs. Once the sale had been completed I was elated because for once in my life I felt that I had achieved something without doing anything dodgy to obtain it.

Now I had more responsibility I put my heart and soul into the business. For me it was what I had always wanted, owning our own home on the coast, it was part of Carol's and mine dream and seeing we were doing well we decided to have our first holiday together, it was to be our belated honeymoon, well, about twenty-seven years belated to be honest. We did not want the usual Spanish holiday that most people were into; we decided to go further afield.

When we landed in Goa, India I just fell in love with the place. What with the heat, the culture and the scenery it was paradise to me. I don't think Carol shared my enthusiasm, but she settled after a few days and we ended up having a whale of a time. It didn't take me too long to find the local brandy which was called Honey-bee and it was very sweet to taste but it could knock you for six with one glass. To cut a long story short, within one week I was drinking two bottles a day and continued to do so for the rest of our belated honeymoon, I even adopted a nickname from the locals 'Mr. Honey-Bee' I would even laugh at myself sometimes when I was called that, but what I didn't realise was that the bastards were taking the piss out of me Mr. Honey-Bee translated from Indian to English means 'You're a fucking piss head mate' and here I was having a laugh at my own expense.

It took three trips to Goa to realise what it all meant and all along I had been thinking that 'These people like me' talk about humiliation I was gutted because I had been giving these piss taker's tips that equalled their wages for a week. That lesson in humiliation taught me one thing and that was that my pride and ego had just taken a battering and I fucking hated it!

My denial of my drinking problem unbeknown to me was huge, but I still thought I could sort it out and drink normally, in fact the following year I took Carol and Josie to Sri-Lanka for the Christmas and New Year. We had booked a five star hotel, all inclusive, which meant as much booze as I could get down my neck. I had given up drinking for the previous five months, just to prove to Carol and myself that I could stop. My return to drinking started again on the flight and within the eleven hour flight I had consumed a bottle and a half of brandy. Once at the hotel we settled in quite well and I soon found my best mate, Aram, who was head barman. My drinking would start around ten in the morning and continue right through to gone midnight. Even Aram, who had seen many heavy drinkers in his time would warn me constantly to try and curb my drinking, but I would say to him 'Hey I'm on holiday and its Christmas and New Year and when I get back home I'll stop again, no problem' famous last words for me, no problem, my arse there wasn't.

After a week we decided to see a bit of the country by means of a tour. Our tour company wanted an extortionate amount for a three day trip so I decided to find someone local to give us a better deal. We were advised not to get a tour locally as a majority of the locals were pro 'Tamil Tigers' and considering they had just blown up the airport in Colombo there was lots of scare-mongering about kidnappings being spread around the resort we were at. After a bottle of Napoleon brandy and a chat with a local geezer on the beach, I came back to Carol and Josie with the good news that we were going on a three day tour in the northern region of Sri Lanka for a tenth of the price that the tour company was asking.

We set off the next day at six in the morning and made our way north, after several stops at temples and plantations we spent our first night in the city of Candy. Our tour guide was a geezer called 'Silver who could speak English but he suffered from a cleft pallet, so he was hard to understand, especially when he was trying to tell us where we were heading. The driver of our air-conditioned van was a geezer of little words, he never spoke English and was darker in skin colour than Silver, yet he could understand what we were saying, so I became a bit wary of him and watched him very closely.

After our night in Candy, we went further north to the tea plantations and opal mines and along the way we went through military checkpoints all manned with uniformed personnel. We took what Silver said was a shortcut to get to a plateau we had wanted to visit and this so called shortcut took hours of driving through dense jungle roads. Carol and Josie were by now getting a bit worried and to be honest I was as well. I asked Silver where the fuck we were heading and he replied that it was a shortcut but with a slight detour because the driver wanted to stop along the way to see his family, so we agreed and I put Carol and Josie at ease by telling them that this was a fantastic experience and that they should be lapping it up, it was all front on my behalf, but I wanted them to feel safe and just said with a smile 'It's great this, in it?' and they just smiled back halfheartedly.

It was now getting dark and we were starting to go through more checkpoints, only this time the personnel were not wearing Military uniforms, these geezers had sarongs' and bandoleers around their necks with AK-47s in their hands. I knew about weapons and realised that the weaponry of the uniformed personnel was different to these geezer's but I never let on to Carol and Josie. It was at these new check points that the non talkative driver started to chat big time with the geezers that were manning them, I also sussed that the language had changed the further we travelled north.

Silver says to me 'John do you want to spend the night with the driver's family as there is a curfew in place?' well what could I say but 'Yeah okay mate because they shoot people out after curfew don't they?' so we continued down these winding mud roads through the fucking jungle until we came into a huge clearing. There must have been at least fifty sarong-wearing men and a few women all sitting around a camp fire eating, the driver was the first out of the van and I watched him go to what I would call the chief, after he spoke to the head man we were summoned out of the van and greeted by the top man who was very friendly and offered us food and drink. There were no chairs or tables, only oblong boxes to sit on and as we sat eating with our hands the top man got up and gave a speech as everyone sat and listened attentively. He went on for about an hour and we never had a fucking clue what the fuck he was going on about. Then the music started and the homemade cashew brew was being passed about, so in a way it turned into a party and boy, did I need that drink.

Josie ask me for the camera so she could snap this great party and as soon as the flash on the camera went the whole lot of them just went manic with AKs at the ready and pointed them straight at us, as quick as a flash Silver jumps up waving his arms and starts talking loudly at the crowd and then he came over to Josie and took the camera off her and then threw it on the fire, once he had done that they all went back to where they left off and the music started again as if nothing had happened. I pulled Silver to one side and said to him 'What just happened Silver?' his reply was quite frightening because he said 'John. These are Tamils and they don't like having their photos taken.' my jaw dropped and I said to him. 'You mean the same Tamil Tigers who attacked the airport a few weeks earlier' 'Yes John the same people, but you are completely safe here, I can assure you'

It was then that I noticed the oblong boxes we had been sitting on because my box contained rocket propelled grenades and Carol's and Josie's were ammunition boxes, I said to Carol 'Don't panic love it's not every day we have an invite to a terrorists' camp' She gave me that look which meant 'What the fuck have you got us into now' I just smiled and carried on drinking the local brew as I knew we had to be seen to be enjoying ourselves. When it came to bedtime we were shown our five-star accommodations which consisted of about five tons of dried elephant shit moulded into a hut, even the bunks were made of it and the smell was unbearable, but what with the aid of the local brew we soon crashed out.

Next morning we were up at dawn and as we wandered about the camp and noticed now that it was daylight Tamils were up in the surrounding trees and had been there all night on watch for Government forces. I managed to get some water down me and sat with a few blokes who were cooking breakfast, I asked what the war was all about and they explained in detail why they were fighting for their independence. Carol and Josie surfaced from the shit huts and came to join us. Carol had not slept at all but Josie conked out due to the drink. Silver came over to us and Carol bit his head off by explaining that her safety was at risk by being in this camp. He did try to pacify her but she was now having none of it and wanted to return to our hotel. After breakfast of fried bananas and eggs we waved our terrorist friends a fond farewell. Carol and Josie were not talking to me because they blamed me for us ending up in a terrorist camp and when she did start to talk, it was all 'We could have all been kidnapped or murdered.' I just said to her 'Look sweetheart it's an experience that I bet no other tourist has experienced. And seeing it was next morning and that we were all in one piece why was she being so long-faced, Josie was okay about what happened to her camera but it was their rules which we had to comply with, no big problem once we knew what we were doing and followed suit.

We left the camp via the checkpoints and drove quite a few hours to the plateau we wanted to visit. It was an amazing experience and we had a great time. After that tour we decided we wanted to get back to the hotel for a good shower and some decent grub plus a nice proper drink, but good old Silver wanted us to go to the botanic gardens which was really nice but bloody boring. It took us 6 hours to get back to our hotel and when the staff saw us enter the reception their faces were a picture. They just stared at us and just looked at us in amazement because the word was spreading that we had been kidnapped.

I made my way to the bar and Carol and Josie went to our room to clean up. While at the bar some of the other tourists asked where we had been, I explained about all the temples, tea plantations and opal mines and then added the Tamil Tigers camp in for good measure. At first they thought we had been lying but once Carol came downstairs and verified our story they began to start to believe us and thought we were crazy. The only regret we had about that trip to the Tamils' camp was that we had no photos to verify our visit, but who cared really after all we knew we had been there and the experience was amazing, even the elephant shit huts.

Coming through customs at Heathrow was no treat for me because I hadn't had a drink since the night before; this was yet, another attempt at controlled drinking. I was sweating and shaking like a leaf as we passed through the corridor with the customs officers either side waiting to pounce on their next victim. We had nothing to worry about so we just started to sail through, that is, until a long arm sticks itself in my path and the owner of it says 'Excuse me Sir! Would you mind stepping over here please?' customs were always polite and straightforward and never kept you hanging around too long, not like the Police, those bastards would have you for a week. He went on to say 'You look unwell Sir, you're sweating and shaking quite badly, have you swallowed anything Sir?' I sussed what they were thinking because I looked like a nervous wreck, which to customs is a good sign to spot drug mules especially if it's their first trip or they were thinking I had something go bang inside my guts from stashed drugs and they were having an effect on me, similar to overdosing.

I replied 'Yeah I've swallowed something and it's made me feel like shit mate.'

'What was that Sir?' he asked eagerly.

I said 'Fucking lamb curry.'

He was now looking at me a bit confused and then said

'What do you mean lamb curry Sir?'

Sarcastically I said 'since having the lamb curry on the flight, I feel like shit mate and if you don't hurry up I'm either going to shit myself or spew up or both right here.'

He started to fluster a bit now because, I don't think he had been taught that one in training college, but nevertheless he had a quick check of our baggage and suggested I get myself to a G.P. and to be honest at that time I did need a doctor because I was actually going into alcohol withdrawal and the ironic thing was, I knew it, but I also knew that another drink would put me right and what with the state of my thinking at that time, it was easier for me to go to the pub then do the sensible thing and go see my Doctor for some form of detox medication. I played with this type of thinking for the next four years and in that time it felt like there was a mini battle going on inside my head.

Things were now getting harder for me to handle, not only on the business front but also my marriage. Carol bless her, started her menopause and I started to seek help regarding my drinking. Carol by then had given me the final ultimatum 'stop drinking or lose me' Carol left with our Josie and moved in with our two sons and I was left on my own with the biggest decision of my life. I started to get help for my drinking problem and after a short while it began to notice. I had by this time stopped for three months and was making all the promises to Carol in the hope she would come back to me.

At four months sober Carol returned to the house with Josie-Lee and it was all happy families for quite a while. I continued to get help for the next two months, then dramatically my thinking changed and said to me 'You don't need this help Johnny boy' so I stopped seeking the help and decided to go it alone as easy as that. Everything went well for the next eighteen months and drink was the last thing on my mind. Through shear willpower and positive thinking I had stayed sober, I quickly forgot about the help I received in the first six months and put my success down to those two fine qualities I possessed. I really did convince myself that drink was not a problem for me but I had to stay sober for Carol, otherwise I would lose her and Josie.

It took all in all two years before I had my next drink and if I am to be honest, I never expected it to happen because on that day I picked up, the last thing on my mind was me sitting in a pub with a beer in my hand. I had been to work that day and all was pucker. I remember getting a phone call from a client who wanted our company to do some work for him and we made arrangements to meet in his local pub, now for me, this was not a problem because I had been in and out of a number of pubs for the last two years without having a single drop of alcohol.

I was sitting at a table with my client looking at the plans for his proposed work and our conversation was in full flow, when out of the blue two pints of lager appeared in front of us, because I was so engrossed in what I was doing I had not paid much attention to the drinks, well not until my client taps me on the arm and says 'Cheers Johnny' as he held his drink to his lips, it was like I was on the outside and looking in on the situation and what I saw was me with the drink in my hand and replying 'Cheers' and taking a gulp from the glass. I remember quite vividly that when I put down the glass on the table I had a quick thought, a thought that was telling me this was not a good idea but just as quickly, another thought came over me and it said 'It's alright Johnny Boy one won't hurt you' sounds familiar doesn't it? Well it should do because it was like a bloody déjà vu to me, been there, got the bloody tee-shirt.

My return to drinking this time was with a vengeance, no matter how hard I tried, I could not stop nor could I do 'controlled drinking anymore but neither could I get pissed, no matter how much I drank. I suppose to others I looked and acted pissed but to me enough was not enough because the booze couldn't get me to that level whereby every problem I had would disappear or be acceptable for the few hours it use to bring and I knew I was in big trouble yet I continued to drink in a vain attempt to get that feel good feeling that normal drinkers get when they have a few. It was at this stage I would start to hide my drink and only drink when Carol was either at work or asleep, I even stayed out of the pubs and bought my booze from different shops from the surrounding area in a poor attempt that the amount I was buying would not be noticed, all crazy thinking when I look back.

To add to the long line of problems I already created, Carol left me again but not for my drinking this time as I have already said I was now a secret drinker. Her menopause was a bad one and with no medication to balance her out she would relive old arguments some as far back as thirty years and I was saying 'sorry' over and over again just to get some peace, but it went from bad to worse with her and our relationship was more like a yo-yo going up and down. This time she walked out again, it lasted for eighteen months and in that time I 'peopled-pleased her and our Josie, on average I would say 'sorry at least ten times a day and to be honest I was getting pissed off with her because she changed into a woman who seemed to get pleasure from hearing me beg for forgiveness' not once did she mention my drinking during this nightmare of a time, every problem she had with me went back to when we were first together, remember, I had been with her since I was fifteen.

Crunch time came for me when I had a phone call from my cousin who had had my Mother staying with her for a family get together on the mainland, but she had to leave early because she was feeling unwell. My cousin explained that she had been trying to contact my mum to make sure she had got home okay. My gut instinct came into play and my thoughts were fully focused on my mother because it was most unusual for mum not to get back in touch and my gut instinct was now telling me that something was wrong. I arrived at mum's house to find it in complete darkness, yet it was nine in the evening. My Mother always worked to a routine since my Father died five years previously and I would know exactly where she would be at all times. I tried knocking on the door and windows but never got a response, by now I had the company of mum's next door neighbour who had the same gut feeling as me. So I decided to break in. This was very easy for me considering my background and I was inside within two minutes without damaging anything. I turned all of the downstairs lights on and saw mum's travelling bag on the floor partly unpacked so I knew she was at home. As I made my way up the staircase to mum's bedroom, I already knew that something was very wrong; I entered her room and found her bed which had been slept in but was now empty then I quickly went into the other bedroom and that's where I found her. She was lying on her back by the side of the bed. I went over to her to check her pulse and as soon as I touched her I realised that she was dead because she was ice cold. I dropped to my knees in shock and just cried out loudly. I was shaking when the neighbour came up the stairs, I told him to contact the emergency services while I stayed with mum. During this time I reflected on my childhood, my mum would always say to me when I put too many problems on her 'You will miss me when I am gone son' and there I was kneeling next to her and knew that she was right.

I was very lucky to have the opportunity to put things right between Mum and me, it came after Carol had done one of her moon-light bunks with Josie-Lee. Mum and me as I mentioned earlier were always at each other's throats, all because she could read me like a book, she was the only one to my knowledge who could and I hated her sometimes for having that ability. We sat down and spoke for the first time and I poured my heart out to her, I told her everything from my relationship problems with Carol, right up to my problem with the drink. We spoke for hours and at all times I was honest as I could be, it felt like a huge burden had been lifted from me, mum spoke of the countless worries I had put her through and on how my Dad would wonder if I would end up dead somewhere. I soon became aware for the first time just how much I loved her. From that chat until her death which was only a matter of months, mum and I got on like a house on fire; it felt so good unloading and getting rid of all the resentments I once had for her and a kind of loving peace developed between us and I'll always be grateful to her for that.

I was sitting in my lounge with Carol sitting opposite me. She had come round once I arrived home after mum had been taken away by the undertakers and in front of me on the table was an unopened bottle of brandy which had been recommended to me by the emergency services because they said I was in a state of shock, they never said to me drink a whole bottle they just said have a couple of drinks, to calm yourself down but my thinking can exaggerate any given suggestion. There I was trying to take in all that had just happened and I knew I had to speak my mind to Carol because our relationship was a joke and I was really pissed off being the 'bad boy,' and the 'yes man,' so I gave Carol a simple choice either you love me and want to come home or we would end the marriage there and then. I told her that I had, had enough of running around after her and just wanted a normal relationship. Carol told me that she loved me very much and wanted to come home with Josie.

That night I was very confused because I wanted to mourn mum's passing but also wanting to celebrate Carol and I getting back with each other so I spun a coin and ended up opening the brandy, the spin of the coin was just a justification for me to drink that bottle because I had already lost the bet well before the coin had been spun. Carol never complained nor did she say anything as I polished the whole bottle off in front of her, 'did I get pissed that night or get to the level of feel-good well being the booze should bring me?' no I didn't, in fact the booze done fuck all for me except give me a bloody headache.

Carol and Josie moved back in and they took over the house instantly. After the funeral things began to improve between us. Carol had been put on hormone replacement which settled her moods for a time but I was still drinking, only this time I was doing it in front of her. She seemed to accept it and we never had any arguments. I often thought what it would be like with Carol and I if I was completely off the booze and decided to try and stop again. After a week without a drink I could feel myself getting all edgy and stressed which meant it wouldn't be too long before Carol and I had a bust up and that was the last thing I needed, so I started up again only this time I came up with a brilliant way of doing it without anyone knowing, I thought that I was the dogs bollocks sometimes with my thinking. When I drank at the kitchen bench at home while on my own I would find myself having these fantastic fantasy ideas on how to get rich quick and I would start with the idea at ten in the morning, by two in the afternoon I was a millionaire and by six in the evening I was bankrupt, all that without moving from the fucking kitchen that gives you some idea where my alcoholism was taking me, I was away with the fairies.

The vibrating alarm woke me at two in the morning; Carol was sound asleep alongside me as I quietly slid out of the bed and made my way downstairs to our dining room. It was there that I had my stash of booze safely hidden out of the way. This was my brilliant plan to drink without anyone knowing. The routine was go to bed at ten and get up at two in the morning whilst Carol and Josie were sound asleep then drink three bottles of 'Chardonnay' and be back in bed by four to get up for work at six, a real smart plan.

I had done this routine for only a short time before a moment of clarity came over me. I was on my second bottle of the night and I was just sitting on the edge of the chair in the dark, I had always sat like that when I was dinking, when I just burst into tears and came over all emotional and full of fear. I was now shaking and crying like a big baby and fell to my knees, as I have said earlier I often prayed for change but this time it was different and I knew it was the right time to ask God for his help. I prayed with total honesty and asked my ship mate to keep the feeling I was experiencing so that when I woke up at six I would still be of the same thinking. I desperately needed help and at that moment of clarity it struck home, I also knew I had to return to the people who had helped me the first time, this wasn't the first time that I had thought of getting help but I would only think of it when I was well oiled but once I crashed out it was forgotten when I awoke and it was this that I asked for, quite simple really, I just asked God to keep the feeling alive and be still fresh in my head when I woke up.

At six in the morning I was up and about, not once did I heave and cough up in the toilet nor was I dehydrated. I looked in the mirror and saw that my eyes were not puffy and bloodshot in fact I felt great as if I had twelve hours sleep and had been on a water diet and 'guess what? That positive feeling was still there and I still felt that need to ask for help. I went off to work that morning and greeted everyone on site with a smile at first they thought I was on drugs then they suggested to me that I may have had a nervous breakdown but the truth was I felt great and kept it up all day. That evening I went back to the people that helped me and as soon as I walked through the doors I knew that this was the place for me, I felt at ease and that fear I should have had was gone. I was greeted with a warm and loving reception from these people and they were over the moon that I had decided to do something about my drinking once and for all.

It did not take me long to accept that I was an alcoholic because I spoke to other people who had so much in common with me, people who had done as I had done and most importantly they thought similarly to me as well. Once I took that on board I felt relieved that I was not the only one who felt like I did. I came back that night and told Carol of my new way of thinking, she was pleased for me but I guess she had heard it all before, only time would convince her. I put everything I could into my recovery and learnt as much as possible about this disease called alcoholism. I have learnt that I have an allergy to alcohol which means to me that one drink is too much and twenty is not enough, it's as simple as that and another thing I learnt is that it is a terminal illness that wants to kill me and there's no cure but with this illness it's not just about putting the bottle down and everything turns hunky dory, there's a lot more to it and that involved change. Carol stayed this time for just over two years, with me being sober throughout. We hardly had arguments or disagreements as I began to change, I thought that I became a loving and caring person again as a husband should be, but that change in me unfortunately was not enough for Carol and she left me yet again with Josie-Lee. I knew what her plans were before she left maybe it was because I was getting used to her routine at leaving.

After six months on my own having no contact with her I had an unexpected call from Carol. She wanted to meet up with me to talk about our marriage. She came to the house and seemed all stressed and anxious. It wasn't too long before I knew of her reasons for being there. She said she wanted us to get back together but I knew Carol was not thinking straight, she wasn't the girl from Peckham I once knew and she wasn't the girl I fell in love with anymore. She said all the things I wanted to hear, she even said she loved me for the first without being asked and she said 'sorry' for the first time in thirty-five years. Normally her saying something like that to me would, without doubt, make me take her back, but my gut feeling was telling me different and the words she was saying were not really meant, after all, I had never known her to speak like this because she was never so affectionate towards me, it was mostly me that took the lead. I asked Carol if she would see a councillor on a one to one basis because it was obvious the reasons she gave for leaving each time were not the right ones and we both agreed there must be other things going on inside her head that needed to be sorted.

We agreed that she would go to the counselling sessions while I was away in India on a building project and then have a sit down chat on my return to see if she still felt the same about me. Three weeks had passed and I never even got a reply to my text messages, so I knew before I got home that she had changed back into Mrs. Hate Johnny. When you live with somebody for that long you're bound to get to know them quite well, but there were more than two sides to Carol and I was about to find out this third side once I was back home. The way she spoke to me was devastating. We had agreed a meet at the back of her sister's shop and as soon as I saw her she looked completely different, her attitude towards me was very arrogant, I remember her eyes, and they had changed into big black saucers and full of hate. I knew there and then that all that we agreed previously was now out of the window and I was about to get it in the neck.

I asked her about the counselling and she told me the Doctor had told her it was not required and then suggested to her to buy a pair of beach shoes and spend the whole summer on the beach which would sort her head out. I asked Carol why she came back to me the last time, when my mum passed away. She paused and stared me straight into my eyes with those big black cold eyes and said 'I only came back because I felt sorry and pity for you John. My heart near on fell out of my arse when she said that, I asked her if it had been my drinking that was making her act this like and she replied with the same tone 'Johnny, you were never a bad drunk.' I knew at that time that this was the end of my marriage and I had a choice.

As I walked away from Carol for the last time my brain was going two to the dozen and the old thinking was trying to creep back in but I was lucky enough to have been warned that this might happen so instead of going to the pub to drown my sorrows I found myself doing something that I thought I would not do in a million years, I walked straight into a solicitors office and started divorce proceedings. I never did get any closure on my marriage which tells me not a lot about my ex wife but I don't blame her for what she done either. Perhaps living with Johnny Mack back then, was that bad, well in Carol's mind it must have been. It is sad that she never took that counselling, maybe if she had then we might have worked it together and been happy today.

I have had to make my own closure on my marriage and I did that by blaming myself entirely for everything and the only way I can make amends for that is to stay sober each day and so far I'm doing okay. I genuinely want Carol to be happy because she deserves what I have been given freely and that's a second chance at life. I was told by someone once that I would lose a lot of things in sobriety but not once did I think I would lose Carol, which just proves to me that we have no control over our direction in life, it's all mapped out for us.

How do I sum my life up? Well that's a hard one. Some people are intrigued with my story and some think it was a waste of life. But from anything negative we can learn to turn that into a positive thing and I do that today by just sharing my story with others. I am today a different person, I love life on a spiritual level and the people in it, I also have a phone book overflowing with friends' numbers, that on its own is a miracle. 'Me in someone's phone directory, don't make me laugh – they would have been the words I would have used to reply to that question a few years ago.

Life is still hard for me even though I have changed my way of thinking, I am slowly going blind with Glaucoma but that hasn't changed my outlook on life or made me pick up a drink. It is so much different today, my attitudes are different and most importantly I have an inner peace which allows other people to have an opinion, but that does not mean that people can walk all over me as some have tried, I just allow others to voice their opinions within reason without me reacting in a negative way, after all we are only human and what someone thinks or says about me is none of my business.

As for my opinions of the people on the Isle of Wight, today they are quite different to when I first arrived on their shores. I have found some great friends here and now realise that it was my arrogance along with my ignorance that made me think the way I did, so my sincere apologies to all of those I slagged off or offended because today I can say that I was wrong.